CHINABERRY HILL

Copyright (c) 2014 Spencer L. Duffy

All rights reserved. Printed in the U.S.A.

No part of this publication may be reproduced or transmitted in any form or by any means, electronic or mechanical, including photocopy, recording or any information storage and retrieval system now known or to be invented, without permission in writing from the publisher, except by a reviewer who wishes to quote brief passages in connection with a review written for inclusion in a magazine, newspaper or broadcast.

Published in the United States by
Beckham Publications Group, Inc.
P.O. Box 4066, Silver Spring, MD 20914

ISBN: 978-0-9905904-2-2
Library of Congress Cataloging in Publication

CHINABERRY HILL

Tidbits of My Life

Spencer L. Duffy

Silver Spring

CONTENTS

Acknowledgments 9
Preface 11

Roots 13
The Early Years 15
Daddy 18
Mama 22
Growing Up As Daddy's Helper 26
Elementary School 32
Middle School 36
High School 45
College Days 48
Assassination of A President 51
Walking With The King 53
Loves of My Life 55
My Stint With Uncle Sam 63
My Second Marriage 84
Retirement Years 88
I Will Build Me A House 91
Commentary On Life 95

To Andr'e my first born and Felicia the baby girl; to my two special daughters, Dianne and Brenda who graciously accepted me as dad after having married their lovely mother, now my wife for 32 years and counting.

I hope as they read the story of my life, they will find tidbits of humor, strength, knowledge, wisdom and perhaps truth that will inspire them to press on toward joy, peace, happiness and fulfillment as they travel the road behind in this wonderful journey called life.

ACKNOWLEDGMENTS

I am deeply indebted to Ms. Delores Henderson (affectionately called Dee) and her voluptuous daughter Monique for preparing the manuscript and to Ms. Jude Andreasen who in spite of her crushing schedule took the time to edit the manuscript and offer her timely comments. Finally, to my loving wife Barbara who produced the art work for the cover. My sincere appreciation for all they did to bring this work to a reality is far beyond words. So I will just say, thank you.

PREFACE

In the left front yard of our house stood a stately, twin-trunked Chinaberry tree. This tree was a haven for me. As the summer breezes passed silently through its pinnately clad branches, the Chinaberry tree spoke; strength and peace to me. In the Chinaberry tree, I saw beauty, grace and a vision of escape from the things that troubled me. In its crook, I kept my stash of hickory nuts, my handmade aquarium and my armory of green Chinaberries, to wage Chinaberry wars with my sisters.

ROOTS

Hello everybody. I am Spencer Lee Duffy, the first of 13 children born to Octavris C. and Leona S. Duffy. I hail from Augusta, (Woodruff Country) Arkansas. Thanks to my brother Edward who researched the ancestral history of our family and is now a professor of Social Studies at Miami Dade College in Miami, Florida, I learned that my African roots run back to an area of the Cameroon on my father's side and to parts of Sierra Leone on my mother's side of the family. I never knew my paternal grandparents. My paternal grandfather passed when my father was only 10 years old. My paternal grandmother was alive when I was born but passed when I was three months old. (In fact, she delivered me.) My maternal grandfather, Mr. Henry T. Stith, was born in 1865. He lived 99 years and died in Saint Louis, Missouri. His first wife (my maternal biological grandmother) died when my mother was a little girl. Grandpop Henry, as we affectionately called him, married a second time to a sweet, quiet and plump lady named Dixie. Although she was not our biological grandmother, she loved and cared for us as if we were her own offspring. How well do I remember her soft lap and gentle touch. It was always a very special time when Grandpop and Grandmamma came to visit us. Grandpop was a softspoken, professorial gentleman. When he came to visit us, he would quiz me on history, art, mathematics and current events. He was an early graduate of Branch Normal College which later became AM&N College and is now The University of Arkansas at Pine Bluff. Like my paternal grandfather he was from a farming background.

I asked my mother, "How in the world did he manage to go to college being poor, black and in Arkansas at such a time in the history of our country?"

She said, "He was a very smart and determined man and once he made up his mind to do something, nothing short of death could stop him."

When Grandpop came to visit us, he always brought his shotgun (at that time you could carry unloaded weapons on the train). He liked his coffee. That was the only time we had coffee in our house. You see, Mama and Daddy did not drink coffee at that time. Mama would prepare breakfast with a pot of strong coffee for Grandpop. I liked the smell of brewing coffee but dared not take a sip because children were forbidden to drink the stuff. When I did get up enough nerve to sneak a taste, I was disappointed. It did not taste like it smelled and it left a funny after taste in my mouth. To this day, I do not drink coffee. Grandpop was a serious hunter. I would rejoice when he would invite me to go hunting with him. I would tag along behind him watching his every move. He would creep quietly and methodically through the woods watching for anything that moved. I remember one time as we emerged from the woods, a covey of quail flew up right in front of us. The noise scared me speechless. Grandpop calmly let them get the right distance from us, raised his 16-gauge Winchester Pump shotgun and brought down a half dozen quail. I marveled at his marksmanship. I was too small to shoot Grandpop's gun but I dreamed of the day when he would come to visit and I would be big enough to shoot his Winchester. Grandpop's health began to fail before he could visit us again. He moved in with my aunt Clydis Mae and her husband uncle Bill where he stayed until his death. I stayed with them for a short time before entering the military. I never knew any of my great grandparents. Information about them is sketchy because they were slaves. Grandpop told me that his father told him that if the white people found that a black child had somehow learned to write, they would cut off his or her fingers.

THE EARLY YEARS

How old do you have to be, before you know you are alive, in the world and a part of the human race? Well for me, it was about two and a half years. You see, I do remember the birth of my first sister, Eliza, aka E. Marie who is about two and a half years younger than I. I do not recall Mama being pregnant. However, I do remember a lady coming to our house one day with a small black bag. Daddy put me and my cousin Gloridine, eight years my senior, in the kitchen which was in the rear of the house. (Gloridine lived with us and was just like a sister to me.) After a long time, I heard a baby crying. I was so excited I bolted to the door but was restrained by my cousin. It seemed like an eternity before the midwife left. I thought for sure that now I could see the baby, but no. Daddy came into the room and told me that I had a baby sister. I asked him if I could see her. He said no, not until tomorrow. Now this was in the afternoon. It seemed like the morning would never come. Finally morning came. I jumped out of bed and headed straight to Mama's bed. Now Mama's bed was no ordinary bed. It set high upon a heavy set of steel springs. It had two ticks (mattresses), the bottom tick was filled with corn shucks and the top one was filled with chicken feathers. It was soft and most comfortable. Sometimes, Mama would allow me to rest in it for a while. It was so high I had to stand in a chair to get in it. By the time I got to the bed, Gloridine was right beside me. I begged her to hold me up so I could see the baby. Gloridine held me up eye level to the bed. I asked Mama to turn the baby towards me so I could see her. She did and I was amazed at my baby sister's hair. Eliza had a full head of black, hairy, worm-like curly hair. I thought babies had very little hair at birth or none at all. I wanted to hold her but Mama said she was too small. I had to be satisfied with a good look. I was so happy that I had a little sister and soon she and I would have fun playing together. At this point I realized I was alive and part of a family.

I was a small baby. Mama said I was so small that she carried me around on a pillow for two months. My head was large in proportion to my body. I could not move my head from one position to the other until I was several months old. Mama said also that I was sickly. I cried a lot and the neighbors said I had 90-day colic. However, Mama thought I was spoiled because when I cried and she picked me up, I would stop crying. I cried a lot at night and my paternal grandmother, who was living with us, made Mama or Daddy get up and walk around with me in their arms until I fell asleep. Mama said for the first three months of my life, one or both of them had to get up and walk around with me in their arms until I fell asleep. Well, Grandmother, bless her loving heart, passed away when I was three months old. Mama told Daddy that Grandmother was gone and so was the getting up at night and walking around with me to keep me from crying. So for the first couple of nights, I cried myself to sleep. After which, I guess that cured the 90-day colic or maybe at that young age I realized Grandmother was gone and could no longer make Mama or Daddy get up and walk around with me to keep me from crying.

I was a happy child and kept close to Mama. Daddy never said much. He never played with me, which was not uncommon for fathers of that time. He seldom called me by my name. The vast majority of the time he would address me as "boy." He would leave the house early in the morning to work in the fields and it would be almost dark before he returned. I was Mama's shadow. I watched her every move as she went about her many domestic chores. I remember her teaching me how to blow my nose, comb my hair, wash my hands, tie my shoes and neck tie and take care of my personal hygiene. When Eliza got big enough, we would play together. Then came two more sisters; Cora C. and Edna Mae; four and six years my junior, respectively. I remember playing with their toys (rag dolls, jacks, mud cakes, and doll houses) as much as I did mine. I guess it was because between the three of them, they had many more toys than I had.

However, I had my share of natural toys made from old wagon wheel hubs, steel rims from old wagon wheels, arrow heads found in the fields and green Chinaberries. I made a bow and arrows from willow branches and cord string, sling shots from forked tree branches and rubber strips from an old car inner tube; and toy tractors from spent spools of sewing thread. I loved to play hide-and-seek and tag with my sisters. I enjoyed listening to Mama and Gloridine read Mother Goose poems to us several times a week, after supper and before bedtime. Although we were patently poor, we enjoyed what we had and we had fun. I remember in spring time, we would go to the meadows and pick wild flowers for Mama. She seemed so happy when we presented our bouquets to her; although, I think she knew our flowers were merely blooms from weeds that grew in the fields.

My early childhood was spent eating, playing and sleeping. These were the glory days for me. I had lots of fun without too much responsibility. I remember building guitars on the side of the house from coke bottles and bailing wire and swings from old plow lines. I caught crayfish from the ditch which ran by our house. I waged Chinaberry and dirt clod wars with my sisters. I had fun with all of my siblings but because my first three sisters were nearer my age, I played more with them. I was away in college when my baby brother James was born. If I had to use a single word to describe my siblings, it would go like this: E. Marie, the dignified one; Cora C., the smart one; Edna Mae, the feisty and gifted one; Henry E. C. (Deceased—rest his soul), the rebel; Leona Marsetta, the quiet one; Bernice, the caring one; O.C. Junior, the diplomat; Edward, the executive; Nancy, the adventurous one; Everlee, the little angel that left us in infancy; Mary, the loving one and James William (omega), the country gentleman. I am alpha, the first one.

DADDY

Daddy was a strict disciplinarian with a drill sergeant's attitude. In fact, I do believe if he had been called to the military, he would have made Master Sergeant—no sweat. He would have been called to serve in World War II but he was exempted because he had too many children to support. He ruled our house with bold and unquestioned authority. He took no mess from us, particularly me. By my being the first child and a boy, I guess he chose to make an example out of me for those who would follow. Daddy was outspoken and did not bite his tongue about his opinions or feelings. Tact was not his strong suit and Daddy had a temper. I remember he had a red mule named Shorty. Daddy said he had mustang in him. After a weekend of rest, Shorty would run around the lot and be difficult to catch and harness. One Monday morning, Shorty was determined not to be caught. Every time Daddy would get near him, he would take off. When Daddy finally caught him, he took him inside the stable (feeding barn) and beat him unmercifully then took him to the field and worked him all day. That broke Shorty from being difficult to catch. From then on, Daddy could walk into the barn lot and say to Shorty, "Woah," and Shorty would stop in his tracks.

Daddy was a good man. He was strong physically and blessed with good judgment. Daddy could sing. He had a strong, clear and beautiful baritone voice. Our church (Jackson Chapel CME, which at this writing still exists as part of the

Chinaberry Hill

United Methodist Congregation) was too small to have a choir. Daddy was the song-leader for the congregation. Many times, at home after work, Daddy would gather us around him and we would have a song fest. These were very special moments for me, for in singing, I could see Daddy's more gentle side. Daddy was a natural leader. He became District Superintendent for the Sunday School. This task required him to travel across the region to the various churches to do business. I remember several times Mama would need wood cut for the fireplace and kitchen stove while Daddy was away. I was too small at that time to help Mama cut wood. So Mama would manage to cut enough to cook our meals. Daddy was active in the community. He became president of the Men's Federation in Augusta and held that office for more two decades. He was a member of the NAACP, the Masonic Lodge (where he became a 33rd degree Mason) and the Farm Bureau. As with other farmers, Daddy spent most of his time tending the farm. In addition to the field crops (cotton, corn, hay and sorghum) we had hogs, cows and chickens. We also had a large garden plot in which we grew most of our vegetables. During the off season (late fall and early winter), Daddy spent a lot of time in the woods, cutting down trees for fire wood for the winter months. Mama would worry a lot when Daddy would go to the woods. You see, felling large trees in the woods is tricky and dangerous because wind shifts can cause the tree to fall in a different direction or lodge in another tree. If it lodged, the other tree would have to be cut down. This complicated the situation and increased the danger. There had been terrible accidents in the woods. Men would get crushed by falling trees or would accidently wound themselves, sometimes fatally, while felling trees or splitting the logs. Daddy was an expert woodsman. He never injured himself or me. He could look at a large tree and tell you where it was going to fall. He would begin the felling operation by sawing a distance into the trunk of the tree on the falling side. Then he would hew out a notch above the saw cut. He then moved to the opposite side of the tree and began sawing at an angle parallel to the notch on the falling side. If it were a very large tree, he would use steel wedges to tilt the tree in the direction of the fall as he sawed. When I turned 10 years of age, I became Daddy's helper. He purchased a single blade 13 axe and a one-man saw for me (Daddy used a double bladed axe) and off to the woods we would go. I quickly learned to chop wood like an experienced lumber jack. Daddy would cut down a large tree. I would trim off the branches, pile the brush and we would stack the logs to be picked up with the wagon later that day or the next day if we stayed in the woods until dark.

I recall the wood gathering experience as one of our most difficult chores. The woods were wet, the weather was usually cold (sometimes, we had to break through ice to get to the trees) and the logs were heavy. We wore heavy rubber (gum) boots and heavy socks to keep our feet dry. Wood cutting kept my body warm but my feet after a while felt like they were freezing. Before long, the pain left and my feet felt like two blocks of ice. I am proud to say that by the time I reached 18, I could cut wood as well as Daddy. The woodsman skills he taught me served me very well during the 25 years in which I owned and operated Duffy's Landscape Service.

Except for work-related matters, Daddy and I never talked much. Perhaps I was afraid to ask him questions about things because of the way I thought he might respond. So I would confide in Mama any concerns I had. Mama always took time to listen to me and give freely her wise counsel and advice. After I left home for college, when I would return for the holidays or semester break, Daddy and I would sit on the front porch and talk a while. However, I never really developed a free and open line of communication with my daddy.

Daddy and our family left the farm shortly after I entered the military in 1957. We had talked about the steady decline in sharecropping and how difficult it was to make it as a small farmer, particularly, if you did not own your farm. During that time, mechanization was rapidly reducing the need for manual labor and the large farms were buying out the small farmers in order to increase their acreage. Much to Mama's and my regret, Daddy never expressed interest in purchasing a farm. Mama tired several times to persuade Daddy to buy a small farm but to no avail. Shortly after I entered the military, Daddy moved our family to town (Augusta). By being single, I had no real need for my military pay. So I sent my allotment to Daddy to help pay for the house. By the time I got out of the military, Daddy had paid for the house. It was a good house but needed a lot of repairs. Now Daddy had good carpentry skills. He practically rebuilt the inside of the house and replaced major support beams for the foundation. He painted the exterior and put on a new roof. Mama still owns the house which is currently occupied by her granddaughter Karen Meshell. While in Augusta, Daddy worked for the city maintenance department. He later took a job as the grounds keeper for Quiet Cemetery on the North outskirts of Augusta. He worked there until his health failed. Daddy lived to be 88 years of age. He died in 1991 and is buried in the cemetery he so proudly kept for many years.

MAMA

*"Mama is sweet, Mama is quiet
Mama is soft spoken, gentle and bright
Mama is cool, Mama is meek
And her love is out of sight."*

Mama has a way of correcting you without scolding, chastising without hostility and loving without condition. Intellectually, I really believe she is the brightest one in our family. Notwithstanding, academically, some of us have attained the highest degree in education. I remember Mama telling me that she could not remember when she learned to read. She said she just picked up one of her sibling's text books and began reading. They did not believe she was actually reading. Rather, they thought she was merely parroting what she had heard from them as they read their books. So they put her to the test. They went and got a book that she had never seen, opened it near the middle, gave it to her and said, now read. Mama calmly took the book and began to read. They were astonished. Mama finished the ninth grade which was the highest grade at her school at that time. After she raised her family (13 children), she returned to high school under the senior's program and graduated an "A" student at the tender age of 64 with two of her sons, O.C., Jr. and Edward. Mama has a way with children, even the unruly ones. She connects with them in a special way. She has a way of calming them down and sitting them down so they can listen and learn from her. After our family moved to Augusta, Mama worked in Augusta Day Care Center and did domestic work for several families in Augusta one of which (Mrs. Gregory) felt our family story was so unusual that she called a journalist (Mr. Joseph A. Blank who at that time worked for the Reader's Digest). Mr. Blank came down from New York in 1976 and took the story of our family and published it in the July 1977 issue of *The Reader's Digest*: The article was titled, "An American Family." I sincerely believe if Mama had the opportunity to pursue a teaching career, she would have been a master instructor in Elementary or Secondary Education. Although she did not reach her potential in the educational field, her teaching skills are manifested in her children. Out of 12 of us, six of us (four girls and two boys) are professional educators. I started down the teaching track, but changed to the technical side of my major (Agriculture) in my sophomore year.

Mama is sweet and easy going but Mama can be tough. I remember one time Daddy was away on church business and Mama saw a man in the field chasing our chickens. The man, who looked like one of our neighbors, had a rifle. Mama calmly went into the house, got Daddy's shotgun and walked out in plain view of the chicken thief. When the man saw mama with the shotgun, he quickly turned and headed into the woods as if he were merely hunting wild game.

Now, I have never seen Mama fire a gun but I believe if the man had aimed at one of our chickens, she would have at least fired over his head. On another occasion, when Daddy was away, we ran out of fire wood for the stove in the kitchen on which she prepared our food. Daddy always had plenty of logs at the wood pile on the side of the yard. This time, there were no logs cut and split for the stove. I was too small to chop or saw wood at that time. So Mama who at that time weighed about 100 pounds (soaking wet), got Daddy's double bladed axe and one-man saw and went to the wood pile, picked out a good size log, sawed it into stove length pieces and split them into perfect stove wood. Now, I had never seen Mama use a saw or axe. I was truly amazed and astonished at her strength. I helped her bring the wood into the house and sat down and watched her prepare our dinner meal. In addition to keeping house, keeping us clean and under control, Mama found time to help us work in the field, even during the time she was pregnant. She would rise at dawn, fix breakfast for Daddy and us (Daddy always had a special breakfast which included some food we did not have), wash the dishes and work with us in the field until a couple of hours before dinner (we now call this meal lunch). She would ring the bell to call us to dinner around mid-day. After washing the dinner dishes, she would join us again in the field and work until quitting time. We would come home, Mama would fix a good supper (we now call dinner), which consisted of pork or chicken and plenty of vegetables from the garden. She and Daddy would talk awhile and if we kids did not have any homework, we would get ready for bed. Mama's health was excellent. Except for pregnancy, I do not recall Mama being sick. I remember she had an accident with a pressure cooker while cooking a hen. The pressure cooker was deep and the hen had to be lifted out with a pair of large tongues. Somehow, while lifting the chicken from the cooker, the tongues slipped and the hot pan with the chicken in it emptied onto Mama's foot. Her foot and ankle were severely burned. She dressed her foot and ankle with some kind of grease and leaves from a weed that grew in the field. She did not go to the doctor who ran a clinic in town. Perhaps it was because she knew how to treat herself or because the clinic was segregated. (The black patients had to wait in a separate small room on the side of the clinic until all the white patients were seen. And if a white patient came in while the doctor was waiting on a black patient, the doctor would hastily finish with the black patient and go see about the white patient, although several other black patients would be waiting. The nature or severity of your medical condition did not matter). Mama stayed in bed for a couple of days. Gloridine, our cousin was big enough to take over the cooking and other domestic chores. Before long, Mama was back at her post as full time mother and wife.

Chinaberry Hill

Mama was always at home. I remember only once when Mama went away. That was when her brother (Uncle Jimmy as we called him, his name was James) was shot in Saint Louis. Gloridine, again took over the domestic chores. We, who were big enough to help, pitched in. Daddy, although appearing to be tough, seemed troubled and sad during her brief absence. In a few days, Uncle Jimmy died and Mama returned home. Uncle Jimmy was a kind and gentle man. He had visited us only a few times before his death. We all were grief stricken at his passing. Mama lived independently in her home in Augusta until she was well into her eighties. When home got too much for her, she moved into a senior citizen's apartment in Augusta where she lived happily for several years. After which she stayed with my second sister, Cora in Little Rock, Arkansas. Now, at the tender age of 100, she resides with my sixth sister, Nancy in Forrest City, Arkansas. She enjoys working word puzzles and reading her Bible. I am careful to communicate with Mama in my handwriting at least once a month and visit her on her birthday which is April 30th. I intently listen to her words of wisdom and still seek her wise counsel. My siblings and I are especially blessed. When it comes to Mamas, "WE HAVE THE BEST."

GROWING UP AS DADDY'S HELPER

When I struck the age of 10, the wonder years of hanging out with Mama and my siblings ended. Daddy told me that I would be with him except when he went to town or out of town on business. He would give me a list of assignments, show me how he wanted them done and expected me to do them well. I thank God I caught on to things easily and could learn quickly. Daddy was quite strict and short on patience. If I messed up once, he would severely scold me and if I messed up the second time on the same task, I got a whooping. Before I got big enough to handle the horses and plow, I was Daddy's water boy. He told me when he wanted his water and how he wanted it—cool. Well, this was not such a hard task. You see, one of my chores was to keep plenty of water in the trough for the horses. So as I pumped water in the trough for the horses, I would wait until the trough was almost full and then fill Daddy's one half-gallon fruit jar with the coolest water the pump could produce. Then I would strike out to the field, where Daddy was plowing which would sometimes be a half-mile from the house. It was hot and sometimes the sand would burn my feet as I made my way. You see, we went bare foot in the summertime. In spite of the heat and hot sand, I would try my best to be on time with Daddy's water because I knew if I was late or the water was warm, I was in trouble.

When the crops got big enough to work, I went to the field with Mama and my cousin Gloridine. Remember, I was still Daddy's water boy. So I had to take a break from the field work (chopping cotton) to take Daddy his water. Sometimes, it seemed he would be almost a mile from where we were working. I would time myself so he would be closest to me when it was time for me to bring him water. He would see me coming and bring the horses to a stop. He would say, with a strong and commanding voice "Woah." I would rush up and give him his half gallon fruit jar of water. He would take a long drag and if it were cool enough, he would smile and say "Aaaah."

If it was not cool enough, he would give me a mean look and say, "Boy don't you bring me any more warm water out here. Do you hear?"

I would reply quickly, "Yes sir" and scamper away before he could strike me with a plow line (a cotton rope-like line used to guide the horses). Until I was old enough to understand the pressure Daddy was under, I thought he was the meanest man on earth.

When I got home from the field, I had to make sure feed was in the stable and water was in the trough for the horses. Daddy would tell me how many plugs (sections) of hay and how many ears of corn to put out for each horse. Their menu would vary depending on their work load. In the early spring when the ground had to be (listed) broken up for planting, the horses were given twice as much food as they were given when they were cultivating the crops. I was also responsible for keeping water in the troughs for the other livestock as well as keeping enough wood cut up for the kitchen stove and the fire place. I also brought the mail home from the mailbox, which set on the side of the road as we walked home from school. The mailbox chore got me into trouble. You see, we walked to school and our mailbox was almost a half mile from our house on the side of a gravel road (Highway 33) that led to the school. Everyday, on the way home, I would stop and look in the mailbox to see if there was any mail. Now, sometimes, we kids would be laughing and playing on the way home and I would forget to look in the mailbox. Well, most of the time, I would remember that I had forgotten to check the mailbox and turn back before we got home. However, this day I did not remember to turn back and check the mailbox.

So when Daddy got home, he asked me if we got any mail.

I replied, "No Sir." For a moment, I really thought I had checked the mailbox but a little later I realized I had not.

Daddy looked at me strange and said, "That's funny, the Kansas City Star always comes on Wednesday." Now, Wednesday was the night Daddy went to prayer band (prayer meeting) at the church. I thought he would take my word and would not bother to look in the mailbox as he returned home. Well, I was wrong. Now Daddy hated lies like God hates sin. If you wanted to get beat up to within an inch of your life, just tell Daddy a lie. That night, when Daddy returned home from prayer meeting, we were all in bed. I heard him coming to our room. My heart sank and began beating so fast; I thought it would burst out of my chest. I knew he had looked in the mailbox and found the Kansas City Star.

He came to the bed, pulled the covers back off of me and sternly said, "Boy, didn't you tell me there was no mail today?"

I quickly replied, "Yes sir."

"Then why was the Kansas City Star in the mailbox when I looked in it on my way home?" Before I could reply, he was on me like white on rice. I was scantily clad in something like a night shirt (we did not have pajamas—those were for well-to-do-kids). With his four inch wide, three foot long, three-ply leather razor strap, he beat me until I laid prostrate on the floor.

He only said as he left the room, "Boy, don't you ever lie to me again." I learned my lesson well and until he died, I never lied to him again.

I remember my last severe whooping. Sometimes, when it rained too much for us to work in the field, we children would play in the house in our room which was adjacent to Daddy and Mama's living/bedroom. It was fun playing hide and seek and other kid games in the crowded room. I distinctly remember one rainy day while we were playing a terrible thing happened. I had religiously saved labels from Kellogg's Corn Flake boxes (corn flakes were a breakfast special at our house; 90% of the times, we had rice). When I had accumulated enough labels, I sent

Chinaberry Hill

them to Battle Creek, Michigan along with $2.00 for a compass ring (a ring with a bubble on top within which was a compass). As a kid, I was always fascinated with gadgets. I never told my siblings I had saved enough labels and money to order it. After I ordered it, it seemed like it took forever for it to arrive. Well, the day it arrived in the mailbox happened to be a rainy day and we were all at home playing in our room. I thought it was a good time to surprise my siblings by opening the package and showing off my compass ring. They all gathered around waiting anxiously for me to open the package and show them my ring. I took my time. I finally opened the package and there it was, a bright and shinny ring with a clear bubble on top under which was an oscillating pointer that would point East, West, North or South as you changed directions. We all were very excited. Naturally, I wanted to test and cherish the ring for a moment alone and without the interference. So I told my siblings to hold off and let me have a few moments alone with my ring. Well, one of my sister's (Edna Mae) could not wait. She kept insisting to see and handle the ring. The other siblings just stood by and looked on anxiously. With a sudden and unexpected move, Edna grabbed the finger on which I had just placed the ring. I instinctively recoiled. However, she had gained such a grip on the ring until when I pulled back the bubble snapped, the compass was ripped off and the ring was destroyed. Instantly and without conscious thought, I slapped her. She screamed as if I were murdering her. Immediately I heard Daddy get up and go over to the wall where he kept his razor strap. Without a word, he entered our room and began beating me as if I had blasphemed against the Holy Ghost. I was 15 years old. Now Daddy had whooped me many times before but this was the mother of them all. It looked like he would never stop. When he finally stopped, he left the room without a word. I lay prostrate on the floor. My back and hind parts felt as if they had been through a meat grinder. When I finally gained enough strength to get up from the floor, I said to myself, this is it. I had three years to graduation. I said to myself, you must strive not to cross Daddy again and to be at peace with your siblings even if it means backing down when they do you wrong. From that day on, I was the coolest and most peaceful child in the family, as was expected of me.

I continued working with Daddy as he did many tasks beyond the regular farm work. I remember helping him drive a new pump in the ground for water when the one we were using went dry (we used pumps instead of wells for our water supply). Daddy was, as were some other men in the community, good at locating a good underground water vein. How they knew how to do it, they would not say. We would build a scaffold-like contraption capable of driving a two inch steel pipe in six foot sections 20 to 30 feet into the ground to the water table. It was a simple but effective mechanism. It consisted of two 12 to 14 foot upright timbers with a heavy wooden block slung between them. To the wooden block, was attached a long rope which passed though a pulley at the top of the scaffold. The contraption stood on a wide wooden base. The base had a hole in it just big enough for the steel pipe to pass through. We moved the contraption into position over which the pump was to be driven. Daddy would hold the first section (the strainer) in perfect vertical position. I would pull the rope and raise the heavy wooden bock to the top of the scaffold. I would suddenly let go of the rope. The heavy wooden block would descend with a thud. It struck the steel pipe with a mighty blow which drove it several inches into the ground. This procedure was repeated until five of six sections of pipe had been driven into the ground. Daddy then attached the pump. We put enough water in the pump to prime it. If the strainer pipe had struck a good water vein, after a few minutes of vigorous pumping, a good stream of muddy water would start gushing from the mouth of the pump. This was good news because if only a trickle or no water at all came out it meant the whole process had to be repeated with a new set of pipes (we had no means of extracting the pipes we had driven). Sometimes, when our pump would get sluggish and produce an inadequate stream of water, Daddy said it was because the strainer had become clogged. He would go get the shotgun, remove the pump from the first pipe, place the barrel of the shotgun as far as it would go down the pipe and pull the trigger. A muffled sound would occur. Daddy would replace the pump and most times it would again operate like new. I learned after I was in college that shot gun pellets were made of lead and after a pump was "gunned," lead pellets remained in the strainer. This meant that the water from a gunned pump contained traces of lead. Apparently, it was not enough to hurt us or the farm animals.

Daddy sometimes made molasses from the sorghum we grew. When he did, he would make molasses for the whole community. The other farmers would bring their sorghum to Daddy's mill for processing. I did not learn to make molasses but I helped him set up the vat, hew the logs to fire the vat and feed the mill. The mill was a simple machine. It consisted of three heavy steel spools that set on a platform. The steel spools were mounted and rotated by a set of gears. The mill was horse drawn. A long pole was attached to the main shaft which extended out of the top of the gear box. The horse was hitched to the other end of the pole and would walk around in a big circle to power the mill. As the sorghum canes were placed between the rotating spools, they were crushed and the juice collected and placed in the vat for cooking. Sometimes, Daddy would let me taste a little of the raw juice. It was very sweet. You could drink only a little of it because too much would upset your stomach.

ELEMENTARY SCHOOL

Leaving home to start my first day of school was not a big deal for me. I was curious to see what school was like. My cousin, Gloridine, had advanced to the eighth grade when I started. She seemed to be okay. So I said to myself, "School couldn't be that bad." I had watched her get up every morning and skillfully fix herself up and dash out to catch the bus. My problem was keeping up with her on the way to the bus stop. You see, Gloridine would primp right up to the nick of time before the bus was to come. Then she would dash out like a racehorse to catch it. I tagged along behind her struggling to keep up.

She would scold me for not keeping up. She would look over her shoulder and holler, "Come on Spencer we are going to miss the bus."

I would become frustrated and angry. I would even cry. However, I would always manage to catch up before we got to the bus stop. When I got to the bus stop, I took the time to wipe the tears from my face so the other children would not know that I had been crying. At that time, kids on the bus would tease you for almost anything that seemed out of order.

Riding the bus was another challenge. You see, I was small for my age (I weighed only 117 pounds when I graduated from high school). My head was rather large and shaped somewhat like a peanut. My classmates would tease me. Some called me long head, rail head and two headed. This made me feel bad.

My father (as other fathers did at that time) cut my hair short. This accentuated the situation. I would tell Mama when I got home from school.

She would look at me, smile sympathetically and say, "Did they hit you?"

I would answer, "No mam."

"Well," she said, "Don't worry. It is what's inside your head that counts. Sticks and stones will break your bones but talk like that won't hurt you."

Sometimes, I would be pressed to my limit and wanted to strike out at them verbally and physically but I remembered Mama's words and held my peace. After a while, the teasing stopped. However, there was another problem riding the bus. The older boys would make it their business to sit behind the younger ones. They would have a field day thumping our heads. Now, by having my big cousin, Gloridine on the bus, I thought she would protect me. I was wrong. Gloridine would sit with her friends, most of the time in front of me and paid little attention to me. I shortly came to the realization that even if she had tried to intercede, those big boys would not have paid her any attention. So I soon figured out a way to limit the head thumping — I would head to the back of the bus if a seat was available. If not, I would sit in front of a girl or a boy near my age.

I soon adjusted very well to school. I remember my first grade teacher. She was short, mahogany, plump and attractive and a very good teacher. All of my elementary school teachers were females. My class was large and our little seats almost touched. They were equipped with a collapsible shelf that served as a writing desk and a head rest for quiet time. I was seated by a little girl. Sometimes when the teacher had her back turned or was writing on the black board this little girl would take my hand and put it under her dress, look at me and laugh. Now at the tender age of six, I was completely innocent and perhaps so was she. She was wearing flower sack bloomers (panties) which was common for little farm girls. I watched Mama make them for my sisters. Although, she thought this funny, I was surprised and felt it was wrong. Luckily we did not get caught. Before long, our teacher re-arranged our seating. I don't remember playing with her at recess (at that age, the boys usually played with other boys). I don't remember her first name but her last name started with an S and ended with an S. I will not name her out of respect for our innocence. I don't know whether her family moved but for some reason, I never saw her again after the first grade.

I was a serious student and had no trouble mastering the first grade. You see, Mama made sure that when we started going to school, we knew our age, and how to spell our name and address. We knew the alphabet, how to count to 100, the Lord's Prayer, the Pledge of Allegiance and the 23rd Psalms. All of my elementary teachers were very good, although some had different teaching methods than others. I remember one in particular: Mrs. Alice Character. She was of fair complexion, wore reading glasses over which she looked at us, carried a foot ruler at all times and had zero tolerance for talking unless you were responding to a question.

She would look up over her glasses and say, "Somebody is talking in here. I know who it is and if they don't stop now, I am going to send this ruler back there."

Well, I didn't quite understand what she meant until I saw the ruler sail right pass my head and land smack up beside the head of the student who was talking. Mrs. Character then asked the student to bring her the ruler. She asked the student to hold her hands out palms up at which time, Mrs. Character gave her several licks in the palms of her hands. That was it for me. I was quiet as a mouse as were 99% of my classmates in Mrs. Character's class.

At the age of 12, I had advanced to the sixth grade. I began to slack off in my studies. I don't know why. Perhaps it was because I had found a very good friend named Judge Jones. I never knew if Judge was really his first name but that's what everybody called him. We could not wait until recess to go crayfish hunting in the ditch that ran past the school. We would remove our shoes, roll up our pant legs, wade into the ditch and begin catching crayfish (now called fresh water lobster). At that time, neither we nor the people in our community knew they were edible. Crayfish are solitary creatures. We would see how many we could catch, put them in a pile and watch them fight. Sometimes, we would be so involved with our crayfish wars that we would not hear the bell ringing to end recess. We would look around and see no one outside but us. We would hurry back into the classrooms, our pants wet and muddy from crayfish hunting. The teacher, Mrs. Jessie Deal, would call us over to her desk, make us hold our hands out and she would give us several painful licks in the palms of our hands with her ruler.

    Mrs. Deal was a soft spoken, heavy-set brown-skinned lady. She called me aside near the end of the school year and told me I was a better student than my performance had shown and that she was not going to promote me to the seventh grade until I went and finished remedial summer school. Now, this hit me like a ton of bricks. I knew I had not done my best but I didn't dream of being held back for remedial summer school. Well, Mrs. Deal was serious. She wrote a note to my parents telling them why she was not promoting me. I was thoroughly embarrassed. Being the oldest sibling, I wanted to set a good example. Now all of my school age siblings at this time were girls so they teased me to no end. I was so afraid Daddy was going to beat me to death. Surprisingly, he had nothing to say. He left it to Mama. I was surprised again, Mama did not scold me or make me feel bad. She told me she agreed with my teacher and for me to go and do better. So, I got real serious with my studies. However, at that time, I thought Mrs. Deal was the worst teacher I had. Now I know she was perhaps the best because she saw my potential and she knew that shocking me would re-focus my thoughts about education. She was one hundred percent correct.

MIDDLE SCHOOL

I entered the seventh grade that fall a new student. I maxed all my homework and was a model student from then on. From the seventh grade through twelfth I was listed among the top students in my class. About this time, tragedy struck our family. I remembered my little sister Everlee. She was a beautiful baby who seemed to be wise beyond her time even at six months, she had a beautiful smile and a brilliant countenance that let you know she was special. One day she and one of my siblings were playing on the front porch. Somehow Everlee slipped from the grasp of the sibling that was holding her. Her head hit the porch's railing. We did not think she was seriously injured. She lost consciousness and Daddy took her to the doctor in Augusta. When he returned, he told us that Everlee had a concussion. The doctor prescribed some medicine and told us to keep her quiet. We did not know what a concussion was. We knew it had something to do with the brain. We all were sad and anxious. Late that night, Everlee died. Now our family had suffered difficult situations before. We had experienced lost crops from floods, sick and diseased animals and run away horses but this was most devastating for our family. This was the first time I saw my Daddy openly express grief. We all gathered around Mama's bed where Everlee was laid. We grieved and cried until the next morning. At daybreak, Daddy went to town to notify the undertakers (funeral home personnel). We all burst into tears when we saw the hearse pull into our yard.

Daddy told me to go and tell our neighbor, Mr. Perry, what had happened. Now I was 17 years old, afraid and grief stricken. How could I tell Mr. Perry? What would I say? I did not want to go but Daddy had given his orders and so I went. As I walked the two miles to Mr. Perry's house, I kept wondering what I would say. Fortunately, when I arrived, Mr. Perry was outside in the yard. He saw the look on my face and knew something was terribly wrong.

He said, "Spencer, what happened?"

I told him my little sister Everlee had died. Mr. Perry went in the house and got his wife. They immediately came over to comfort us and help arrange for Everlee's burial. The preacher came and gave a short ceremony at our home. Everlee was buried in a grove of trees near the back of the farm.

Only one man in our community had a car. His name was Mr. Pick Herd. Everyone called him Pick. I do not know if that was his real name or a nickname but that's what everybody called him. On rare occasions when we needed to go to McCrory (the next town—about 12 miles from Augusta) Daddy would contact Mr. Pick. He would come in his 1930 vintage Ford. We would all crowd in and head to McCrory. I don't remember why we had business in McCrory but I do remember watching Mr. Pick drive. I was curious about how he seemed to fight with the steering wheel to keep the car on the road. I learned much later as I entered auto mechanic's school that Mr. Pick's car had a badly worn gear in the steering box which caused excessive play in the steering wheel. Therefore, he had to over steer to make minor steering corrections as he drove.

When days grew cold and snow began to fall, food, particularly meat, became scarce. Although we had killed hogs, we needed other meats to supplement our winter meals. Daddy showed me how to make a "dead fall." This contraption consisted of a wooden platform above which was attached a heavy weight. The weight was connected to a strong cord. The platform was attached to a window seal. The heavy weight was hoisted above the platform by the strong cord. The cord was anchored to a nail inside the window. The platform was then covered with crumbs or some kind of grain. Pretty soon the platform would be covered with birds. I would suddenly release the cord from its anchor. Down came the heavy weight with a crushing blow. A few birds on the edge of the platform would escape but most of them would be killed. After repeating this process a few times, we would have enough meat for dinner. The poem "sing a song of six pence, pocket full of rye, four and twenty black birds baked in a pie" became a reality. The harvest from my dead fall provided much appreciated meat for the cold snowy, winter months.

 Daddy, like Grandpop, was a good hunter. He would take his 12-gauge double barreled shotgun along with a large shoulder (gunny) sack which Mama made from old cotton sacks. He would strike out to the woods. Mama would become anxious if he had not returned by dusk dark. He always returned. Most of the time he would emerge from the woods with a sack full of rabbits, squirrels or other wild game. At the time, I was too small to follow him but I was big enough to help dress them. Mama would cook them. She knew how to fix them just right. Sometimes she would fix them with gravy or dumplings. When the vegetables she had canned were added, we had a very wholesome and delicious meal.

 When I got big enough to go hunting with Daddy, I became his scout. I carried a long stick and kept a sharp eye out for any movement in the bushes. If I saw or heard anything, I would run over and beat the bushes until whatever was in them ran out. We had a dog that would sometimes go hunting with us. However, the dog was gun shy. He would hunt very well until he heard the first shotgun blast then he would turn tail and run home as fast as he could. Daddy would just shake his head. I thought it was funny. I soon grew tired of scouting for Daddy. So I asked him if I could take the gun and he do the scouting. He said no because I was not strong enough to stand the recoil from a 12-gauge shotgun. Well, one day when Daddy was away in town, I decided I was going hunting by myself. So, I took his 12-gauge double barreled shotgun which always set in the corner of the living room, and headed for the woods. I was excited and looked for anything that moved. After a while, a rabbit jumped up a short distance from me. I took the stance like I had seen Daddy take. I aimed but in my excitement, I pulled both triggers. The recoil hit me like a ton of bricks. My heels went up, I fell backwards on my back side, the shotgun jumped out of my hands and the rabbit got away. I quietly picked myself up, retrieved the shotgun and returned home. I put the shotgun back in its place and never told Daddy or Mama what I had done.

I was always anxious to learn and curious about how things worked. I had no money to go to college, neither did my parents. So, I had to figure out a way to earn enough money to pay for my first semester in college. I developed an entrepreneurial spirit by age 10. I would order garden seeds from a wholesale catalogue out of Lancaster, Pennsylvania. Each spring, I would sell them retail to the neighbors in the community. At age 16, I got a Western Flyer Bicycle for Christmas. The following spring, in addition to selling garden seeds, I opened a paper route. Our community had a radius of about five miles (all dirt roads). Saturday mornings, I would get on my bicycle, trudge over the sandy dirt roads and proudly deliver *The Chicago Defender*, the major weekly national African American newspaper, to most of the neighbors in the community. In addition, I begged my father to give me a little plot of land to raise a garden from which I could sell vegetables. He agreed but told me in no uncertain terms that my personal garden did not exempt me from any of my regular chores including working our regular garden.

I said, "Yes Sir. I understand." I was happy to have an opportunity to earn money. I successfully raised several vegetable crops. However, my main crop was greens (mustard and turnips). Daddy allowed me to raise chickens and sell them to the towns-people. So with my vegetables, frying sized chickens and my bicycle, I had a mini mobile farmer's market. We worked the farm Monday through Friday and except when we got behind because of bad weather, we were free on Saturdays. When we worked on Saturdays, it was only a half-day. This compressed my delivery system. I would scramble to my garden, pick my vegetables, collect my fryers on foot (I sold them live) and rush to town. I managed to make my sales and return home before dark. I had a steady stream of regular customers. They would place their orders on Sundays by seeing me in person at church or by sending word by a neighbor. You see, we had no telephones.

The chickens were a part of a 4-H project. Daddy and Mr. Henry Smith, our County Extension Agent, were good friends. So I saw him when he came to our home to give Daddy USDA (United States Department of Agriculture) information or discuss Farm Bureau matters. Mr. Smith was also our 4-H Club advisor. The 4-H Club was similar in principle to the Boy and Girl Scouts for city children. It emphasized good citizenship and equal training of the Heart, Head, Hands and Health, thus the 4-H. I told Mr. Smith I wanted to go to college but had no money. He had observed my success with my vegetable garden and newspaper route. So, he suggested that I raise frying sized chickens to sell. I was happy to have the opportunity. Mr. Smith assisted me in constructing a brooder (a special pen for raising broilers). This pen consisted of an enclosed shed with a screened-in sun porch. It was heated with a kerosene lamp. Mr. Smith would sometimes take me home with him to help his beautiful wife with domestic work. I remember one time while I was helping in the house. Mrs. Smith was boiling something on her gas stove. (Many people at that time were afraid of gas stoves because they had heard they would blow up.) I had no experience with them, so I was suspicious. Well, something in Mrs. Smith's pot boiled over. It ran down onto the gas burner. It made a hissing sound and the flame turned yellow and flared up. I was horrified. I just knew that stove was going to explode. Mrs. Smith saw that I was frightened out of my wits. She calmly removed the pot from the burner and explained to me how the stove was designed to handle boil-overs and that gas stoves were very efficient, reliable and safe. With her reassurance, before long, I gained my composure and continued my work.

In late fall, after most of the cotton was picked, the corn pulled, the hay raked and placed in the barn, Daddy would pile us in the wagon and head to town. Now, there was only one department store in Augusta called Bill Reeves. He had one clerk, a lady whose name I don't remember, but she had a voice like Mini Pearl of the Grand Old Opera. Her eyes would light up when she saw us coming.

She would call to Mr. Reeves, who would be in the back of the store, and say, "The Duffy's are here."

He would come out and greet Daddy and look us over. He would say to the clerk, "Fit the kids with whatever Duffy wants and call me."

We each would try on several pairs of shoes which Daddy had selected and when a pair fit, we would give them to the clerk. She would box them and set them aside. The process continued until we all were fitted.

She would then call Mr. Reeves. He would come out and say, "Duffy, do you have all the kids fitted okay?"

Daddy would reply, "Yes Sir." Then he and Mr. Reeves would go to the back of the store to Mr. Reeves' office. After a while, they would emerge, the shoes we had selected would be packaged and we would head for home. I never knew whether Daddy paid Mr. Reeves in cash or whether he put our shoes on credit (Mr. Reeves would extend credit) but we always got our shoes.

Daddy told us in no uncertain terms that we would get no more shoes until the next fall.

That we were responsible for protecting and maintaining our shoes and if we wore them out before the next fall, we would have to go barefoot everywhere, including school and church. So, I made sure I protected and maintained my shoes and did not abuse them. During the summer when school was out, we went bare feet except when we went to church or town on a special occasion. Occasionally, in spite of my best efforts, I would wear a hole in the sole of my shoe. Well, I had a remedy for that. I simple cut a piece of paste board (card board) to fit like an insole, placed it inside my shoe and kept on stepping. Of course, I was careful not to cross my legs in public. However, I could not hide the hole in my sole when we knelt around the altar for prayer or communion. So, while I prayed, I also prayed that the worshipers on the front row would be so consumed by the Holy Spirit until they would not notice the hole in my sole.

Spencer L. Duffy

We had two favorite first cousins, James Ellis and Florida Mae, aka Florita, who lived in Chicago. Their father, Uncle Ishmael, would sometimes bring them to Augusta to spend the summer with us. I would be very happy to see them, particularly James because he was three years my junior but as big as I. He was curious about the country and the farm. I took great pride in teaching him about the horses, cows, pigs and chickens. Our favorite sport was climbing. When we were not working in the fields, James and I would head to the woods, pick the highest tree we could find and climb to the top. James was quick in learning to climb. I would shimmy up the trunk of a large tree until I reached a limb and James would be right behind me. If we found a tree that was tall enough, when we reached the top, we could see the Blue Ridge Mountains (a part of the Ozark Mountain Range that runs through Arkansas). We enjoyed the sights and the heights. I taught him how to move from one limb to another, to be sure the limb was not rotten and that it was big enough to support his weight. We became expert climbers. Now there was a peach tree in the cow pasture a short distance from the yard. The tree was loaded with ripe peaches. Some had fallen to the ground. Some were hanging low enough to be picked from the ground. As is commonly known, the best fruit was near the top of the tree. James fixed his eyes on several lush peaches hanging out on a limb near the top of the tree. I warned him that I thought the limbs were too small to support his weight. I begged him to settle for some of the low hanging fruit or for some of the nice peaches on the ground. He would not listen to me and proceeded to climb the tree in hot pursuit of the prime fruit near the top. James was doing fine.

He was almost in hand reach of his prized peach. He had positioned himself in a standing position facing his prized peach. In this position, he could hold onto and upper limb with one hand and pick his peach with the other hand. I forgot to tell James that often wasps made their nest in fruit trees so they would easily get the ripening fruit. Well, just as James was far out on a strong limb and reaching for his prize peach, his head bumped into a wasp nest. James began fighting the wasp away from his head with both hands. He turned around like a tight rope walker and began running back toward the trunk of the tree. Now, I have never seen a person run down a limb of a tree without holding on to anything. He almost made it. His left foot slipped and he fell to the ground. Luckily, the limb was not very high. The wasps left when James hit the ground, but not before they stung him many times. He jumped up holding his head, obviously in pain. I was laughing so hard that I could not speak or comfort him.

When he got his breath, he shouted to me, "Why didn't you tell me there were bees in that tree?"

I said, "I did not know that they were there, and they were not bees but wasps that stung you. Furthermore, remember I told you to settle for the low hanging fruit or some that was on the ground."

By that time James' head was swelling. We forgot about the peaches and headed for Mama. I told Mama what happened.

She just smiled, went and got some of Daddy's tobacco, made a paste and put it on his head. Before long, the swelling began to go down. We went back to playing but not near the peach tree. We were so confident with our climbing until we decided that trees were not tall enough. Now, White River is right outside of Augusta city limits. So, we decided to ride double on my bike to the foot of the White River Bridge and climb to the top of the superstructure. We parked my bike on the bank of the river near the foot of the bridge (neither one of us could swim). We followed the guard railing to where it connected with the steel superstructure. I began climbing with James right behind me. I told James not to look down until we got to the top. Now White River Bridge is not a low bridge. The superstructure must extended 100 feet or so into the air. I continued climbing with James a few feet behind me. I had almost reached the last rail when a loaded tractor trailer came barreling over the bridge. The superstructure began shaking violently. We were afraid. I told James not to look down and hold tight until the truck passed. (I had no idea bridges shook like that when bearing a heavy load.) The truck passed. I took a deep breath. We forgot about looking out to see the Blue Ridge Mountains or anything else. All we wanted to do was get down off that bridge. Well, we made it down, got back on my bike and headed home. From then on, we settled for climbing trees. I never told Daddy or Mama what we had done.

I longed to be delivered from the darkness that surrounded me in Augusta, my home town of about 3,000 citizens. I wanted to leave the ignorance and prejudice that over shadowed my community and shunted my dreams. So, at age 15 I made up my mind to prepare myself to leave Augusta, Arkansas. First, I said I would not tell anyone including Mama, with whom I felt comfortable talking about anything. My plan crystalized while sitting in a math class taught by Mr. H. Milliard, who was a very good teacher. He always carried a yard stick which he used as a pointer for the black board. It was a summer day, the windows were open (we had no air conditioning) and a bee flew in the window. Mr. Milliard was putting a problem on the board.

He was writing with one hand and the yardstick was resting on his shoulder while being held by the other hand. Without a pause or without moving the yard stick from his shoulder, with a slight cool horizontal stroke, he knocked the bee back out the window with the same speed with which the bee flew in.

At that moment, my plan crystalized. I said to myself, "You must absorb every ounce of knowledge imparted to you by your instructors. You must be obedient to your parents and you must find a way to get enough money to enter college." Mama had told me many times that education was the key to freedom and success.

HIGH SCHOOL

I am a senior now. We lived a little more than a mile from the school. You see, our school was in a single two-story building. Grades one through six were taught on the first floor and grades seven through twelve were taught on the second floor. You could see the tin roof of our house from the second floor. It was a clear day in May about two weeks before graduation. Someone came into our classroom and said a house was burning. I looked out of the window and saw a huge plume of black smoke billowing over the trees. My heart sank. From the location of the smoke, I knew it was our house. I called my best friend, Judge Jones, who happened to have driven his father's car to school that day.

I said, "Judge, I think our house is on fire. Will you take me home?"

Without hesitation he said, "Let's go."

We jumped in his car and within three minutes, we were home. When we turned off the main road into the lane leading to our house, I could see the walls were collapsing. Our house was rapidly burning to the ground. I jumped out of the car before it came to a full stop and started yelling for Mama and Gloridine. Mama heard me and called back from the vacant house which set about 50 yards from our house. I ran over and found them huddled together and crying.

Mama, sobbing, said, "Spencer, we have lost everything."

I said, "Mama that's all right. We can get some more stuff. I am so glad that you, Gloridine and the baby got out safely."

Mama said it was windy and she was in the kitchen and Gloridine was out back. Although it was May, it was cool and there was fire in the fireplace. Somehow, the front door blew open and blew the hot embers from the fireplace onto the wood floor and the floor ignited. Gloridine saw the fire coming from the front of the house and ran in to tell Mama the house was burning. The baby was asleep in the living room where the fire started. By the time Mama came from the kitchen to the living room, it was engulfed in flames. Mama rushed into the burning room with Gloridine holding to her apron and snatched the baby from the burning bed and they ran out though the back door. Mama attempted to go back into the house to try and save some of our belongings but Gloridine restrained her. (As rapidly as our house was burning, I do believe if Gloridine had not restrained Mama, she would not have made it out.) Daddy was plowing in the lower field behind a scope of woods about a half mile from the house. Mama told me to go tell Daddy our house had burned down. I took off to where Daddy was.

When he saw me coming he brought the horses to a halt and before I could speak, he said, "Our house burned down didn't it?"

I answered, "Yes Sir." He asked me if anybody got hurt. I said, "No Sir."

He unhooked the horses from the plow and we came home. By the time we got home, our neighbors and many of the school teachers had arrived. For the first time, our family had to be separated (there were too many of us to stay in one place). I stayed with my third grade teacher, Mrs. Raspberry. She lived on Highway 64 just outside of Augusta city limits. Although the Raspberry's home was neat and comfortable and they did what they could to console me, that night was long and mostly sleepless for me. Our family was apart only for one night. The next day, Daddy came and got me and we patched up the old house that was a short distance from our burned house. He furnished it with bedding and furniture donated by our neighbors. Daddy hooked up the wagon and we went around the neighborhood collecting my siblings. We rejoiced to be together again in spite of our loss.

I graduated a couple of weeks later as valedictorian of my class. In my speech to my fellow classmates, I reminded them of the challenges we would face as we made our mark in a rapidly-changing world. I also reflected on the fun we had and the love for our teachers and Carver High School. A few days before I left for college, Mama sent me to town to pick up some groceries. The owner of the store was named Cecil Willis. He saw me struggling with a large bag of groceries so he offered me a ride home. He had an almost-new car and I was glad to get a ride. He knew I had graduated from high school. He asked me what I was going to do. I quickly replied that I was going to college. He seemed to be stunned.

After a long pause, he said, "Boy you don't need to go to college. You need to stay at home and help your father work the farm."

Now, I was taught to always be respectful to adults, particularly to those of the caucasian persuasion. It took all of my mental strength to keep from giving Mr. Willis a piece of my mind in words that you don't hear in Sunday school. So, I bit my tongue, gave him a long and frigid stare and never said a mumbling word. When we got home, I thanked him for the ride, collected my bag of groceries, got out of his car, slammed the door soundly and went into the house. I never saw Mr. Willis again.

COLLEGE DAYS

When I became a senior in high school, through my entrepreneurial projects, I had accumulated a substantial amount of money which I had planned to use to get into college. As fate would have it, I kept the money at home and it burned with the house. Mr. Smith, our county agent, knew my perilous situation and came to my rescue. He told me if I really wanted to go to college, he would talk to one of the professors in the Agriculture Department and see if he would hire me for the summer. (Customarily, summer work is reserved for continuing students.) I was so excited at this offer. I thanked Mr. Smith again and again. Mr. Smith went to AM&N College (now The University of Arkansas at Pine Bluff), that weekend and talked to Mr. O. R. Holiday, a professor of Animal Husbandry in the Department of Agriculture. Mr. Holiday was in charge of all domestic livestock on the research farm including the swine. I could not wait for Mr. Smith to get back to me with the news about my summer job at the college I wanted to attend. In a few days, Mr. Smith came to our house and told me that Mr. Holiday had agreed to hire me for the summer. I was simply overjoyed. I thanked him copiously and told him I would work hard and do a good job.

  The next week, Mr. Smith came for me. I had my few things packed in a cardboard suitcase. I had $25.00 in my pocket. I said goodbye to Mama and the rest of my siblings (Daddy was not at home). We took off for Pine Bluff, Arkansas (about

Chinaberry Hill

120 miles from Augusta). We arrived in the afternoon. Mr. Smith took me to the Agriculture Department to Mr. Holiday's Office. Mr. Holiday was at his desk. He was a dark, tall and distinguished looking gentleman. He greeted us warmly when Mr. Smith introduced me. Mr. Holiday asked me if I had any experience working with hogs. I replied, yes Sir, and that I had worked on the farm with Daddy's hogs since the age of 10. Mr. Holiday and I connected right away. He took me to the college farm and showed me the swine pasture, complete with farrowing pens, feeding stations, a storage shed and an abattoir (slaughter house). We returned from the farm. I was shown my room in the dormitory (some other students were working for the summer, so I was not alone).

It was a small room with bunk beds, a dresser, and a small table. I was elated to have my own private room for the first time in my life. I was very happy. I thanked Mr. Smith again as he left. I had a hard time sleeping that night. I was excited and could not wait to get started on my summer job. Daddy had done a super job of training me to work. I got started Monday morning and found the job to be quite easy compared to my work at home.

After working for about a month, I decided to organize the swine department. I did not tell Mr. Holiday what I had planned to do. First, I named all of the adult hogs including the boar. Then I gave each of them a control number. I kept a journal of their weight, feed consumption, and made notes of their behavior. I kept a record of the sow's breeding dates and the number of pigs born to each of them. Mr. Holiday was very pleased with my work and impressed with my ideas. In fact, he told me that I had drawn up the same plan that he was going to implement that summer. I was delighted to know that we thought alike. I worked full-time from May to September and accumulated enough money to enroll in my freshman semester. I continued to work with the swine after school but on a part time basis. My last class was at 3:00 pm. That left two to three hours for me to complete my chores with the swine. Mr. Holiday was very pleased with my work. Before long, I had no problem getting work after class or on weekends anywhere they needed help on campus.

During my freshman year, I met Mr. J. M. Cheatham, a professor of Agricultural Engineering. He was a heavy set, a light-complexion, jolly man. He seemed to have a way of making complex problems simple. He was industrious. Many times, on weekends, I would go with him and assist him in wiring or making electrical repairs to houses in Pine Bluff. I became his number one assistant. I would go to his home or to his farm in Homer, Louisiana to repair fences or do other farm chores. I remember helping to build steps and sheds and also hang doors at his home. His wife was a lovely lady and an excellent cook who always fed me when worked for them. I remember she decorated her home with antique furniture. I remember at one dinner meal she served what I thought was steak. Mr. Cheatham kept asking me if I liked it.

I replied, "Oh yes sir. It is delicious" He smiled and asked me if I knew what kind of meat I was eating.

I replied, "Beef steak of course."

He said. "No, you are eating venison." He told me how he had prepared it.

"Well," I said, "It is just as good as steak."

My college days were some of the best times of my life. Once I got used to the campus and study requirements, I had no problem. After my freshman year, I was on top of my course work and consistently made the dean's list. I kept a low-profile social life in college. My work and study schedule seriously limited my social activities. My first serious courtship began my senior year. I became active on campus and by the beginning of my senior year, I ran for and was elected president of the student government.

ASSASSINATION OF A PRESIDENT

I never dreamed that I would live to see my beloved country sink so low as to allow the murder of a sitting president. I had read about the assassination of Abraham Lincoln and William McKinley in my history studies. It was in the fall of 1963. I was a graduate student at Howard University. We were in the laboratory, hard at work on our various experiments in plant physiology. One of my colleagues from Alabama, an attractive and jovial young lady, burst into the laboratory and said, "The president has been shot!" At first, we paid no attention to her because she had a habit of joking. When she repeated it in a more somber tone and with a saddened countenance, we realized she was not joking. We all stopped what we were doing, shut down our equipment, gathered our books and left the laboratory without a word. I returned to my apartment, which was a short walk from the campus, tuned in to an all-news radio station and heard the announcer say that the president had been shot in Dallas Texas and had been rushed to the hospital in critical condition. Before too long my worst fear was realized. Classical music was playing and then the announcer broke in and said that President John F. Kennedy had died from his wounds.

I was shocked beyond words. Except for classical music on the radio and television, there was an eerie silence everywhere, even in the streets. I wondered, with all the presidential security, modern equipment and intelligence, how such an awful thing could happen in America. A little more than a week later, President Kennedy's body was laid in state in the Capitol Rotunda. The line of viewers stretched from the Bethune Memorial in Lincoln Park all the way to the Capitol. I stood in line all night, holding my infant son, Andre' in my arms and supporting my wife Bobbie by my side. At about daybreak, we were within a block of the Capitol. My wife grew weary and said she could stand no longer. We gave up and came home and watched the viewing on television.

It was a very sad time for America. I realized how one demented mind could escape the iron grip of federal security, bring down a sitting president and change the course of history.

WALKING WITH THE KING

I missed two opportunities to see Dr. King while attending graduate school at Howard University. One time at Cramden Auditorium where Dr. King was speaking, I arrived about a half hour before time thinking I could get a seat. Now, this was at the height of the Civil Rights Movement and crowds followed Dr. King like they follow rock stars today. To my surprise and dismay, I could not get into the auditorium. The crowd had spilled over to the outside. So I listened on the outside from afar.

Then came the march on Washington in August, 1963. I arose early that morning, went over and picked up my friend, Liston Legette and we drove to within a few blocks of Constitution Avenue and parked. It was a beautiful day. We began walking toward the Lincoln Memorial. The crowd thickened exponentially as we walked. By the time we were in shouting distance of the Lincoln Memorial, I found myself in a sea of humanity. I could not move except in the direction the crowd was going. For the first time in my adult life, I felt helpless. I had no choice but to go along with the crowd. I prayed I would not fall. We stopped about a block from the reflecting pool. A sea of people filled the mall all the way from the Lincoln Memorial to the Capitol. Some ambitious young men were perched in trees along the way. Dr. King's strong and eloquent voice boomed over the speakers. The crowd fell uncommonly silent and listened intently to every word of his most noted speech, "I Have A Dream."

I realized that I was experiencing history in the making and that neither I, nor any of those attending this march would ever be the same. I returned home and watched the recap of the march on the evening news. The reporter said that the crowd was peaceful, there was no violence and the number gathered was estimated to be over 200,000.

Dr. King was assassinated in Memphis, Tennessee in the spring of 1968. Washington, D.C. convulsed into rioting, burning and looting. I could see the flames from the Beltsvillle Laboratory where I worked. I had to negotiate my way through angry crowds of people who wanted to use my new truck to transport their looted heavy appliances such as refrigerators and televisions from the stores to their homes. It was a sad and frightening time to be in Washington.

LOVES OF MY LIFE

I am grateful to all of my girlfriends. Each, in her own way, added spice, excitement, adventure and sometimes special challenges to my life. Many of them are still alive. Therefore, their names have been cryptographically abbreviated.

Ms. S.E.: High school sweetheart—Cute, smart and an extrovert. We never got serious about our relationship. We were more like good friends. I may have stolen a kiss once or twice. I would see her briefly at recess, hold her hand and escort her back to class. I let her wear my class ring. In fact, I never retrieved it after graduation. After I left Augusta, I never saw her again.

Ms. S.C.: Serious, pleasingly plump and easy going. We never got too serious but we had a solid relationship. I would visit her on weekends, but I was financially impotent. Therefore, I could not take her out to dinner or the movies. So, we spent a lot of time at her house. I would kiss her gently and go back to my dormitory to resume my studies. Before long, we drifted apart. She found another boyfriend with better financial resources and I was alone again. Being the first sibling, I had no one to follow in boy girl relationships. So, I had to find my own way. I was shy also which exacerbated the situation. I was a late bloomer and had to learn the mechanics of courtship and the complexity of the female emotions. After I got the hang of it, I did just fine.

Spencer L. Duffy

Ms. F.A.: Flashy—Slender built and very social. I felt very comfortable with her. She lived in the dormitory and was a class behind me. We would meet after class sometimes in the Student Union Building. I would walk her through the Bell Tower (a favorite spot for courting couples). We would pause a while and talk. I would kiss her warmly and walk her back to her dormitory. Sometimes, on the way, I would serenade her. She said I sounded like Nat King Cole. We got pretty tight. At that time, I had a part-time job on campus as a mail carrier. I would make two trips a day down town to the main post office, pick up the college mail and deliver it to Mr. Stephens, the campus post master. I had access to his personal car which I used to pick up the mail. I always parked Mr. Stephen's car near the Student Union Building after my evening delivery. Now, the post master's car was only to be used for official business. We had attended a dance in the Student Union Building. I told my girlfriend that I was going to take her to lover's lane after the dance. She said okay. It was a beautiful summer night. The sky was exceptionally clear, the stars looked like diamonds and a full moon lit up the night. After the dance, we jumped in the post master's car and headed to lover's lane, about two miles off campus down a narrow tree clad dirt road. We talked briefly. We began to pet. Things got steamy. We moved from the front seat to the back seat of the car. She became passionate but hesitant as I pressed her for intimacy. Now at the age of twenty, I am a victim of raging hormones. I felt we had passed the point of no return but she became more resistant. I could not or would not let up.

She pulled me close to her and whispered in my ear, "It is the wrong time of the month."

Now that thought had never entered my mind. I first thought she was kidding but I soon saw that she was serious and was telling the truth. Well, it took me a while to return to normal. After a while, I kissed her sweetly, drove back to the campus and walked her back to her dormitory. We courted for the rest of that year. When school was out in May, she went home. I stayed on campus to work full-time for the summer. By the beginning of the fall semester, we went our separate ways but remained good friends. I wonder why she did not tell me it was a bad time of the month before I illegally took the post master's car and drove all the way to lover's lane, Well, I guess she was too modest or perhaps she thought we were just going to talk and pet.

In my junior year, I decided to lighten up on the girls and concentrate on my studies. Now enters Ms. C. U. This young lady caught me by surprise. She came to me for some advice on personal matters. By this time, I had become president of the Student Government. I was impressed with her modesty and intelligence. I did not see her becoming my girlfriend but as we talked, I was strangely attracted to her. After counseling her several times, I asked her if she lived on campus. She said no, she lived at home a couple of miles from the campus. Sometimes, she would catch the bus to the campus but most of the times, she would walk to school. I asked if I could walk her home and she said yes. We walked and talked. I met her mother and sister, who both like her were kind and gracious. She began to grow on me. During my senior year, we got engaged. I graduated and shortly afterwards went into the military. We hooked up again in Washington D. C. after my discharge from the army. Within three years, we were married. There was no shortage of love between us, however, there were some things on which we just could not see eye to eye. I was a man on fire, full of energy and ambition. I had set a goal of accumulating enough wealth to retire at age 45. I was 29 and she was 26 when we got married. She was a good wife and mother, quiet and somewhat of an introvert. By the time I realized our marriage was in trouble, it was too late. Bobbie had given up on me.

One day, while at work in the laboratory, I received an emergency phone call from my landlord (I am now employed with the Agricultural Research Service in Beltsville, Maryland). His voice was stressed as he told me that a U-haul truck was backed up at my front door and my family was being moved out. I thanked him and told him I would meet him at the house. I got in my car and sped home only to find my house empty except for a small card table and a bed. I assured Mr. O'Brien that I was not running out on him and that I was surprised and sorry for what had happened. I told him we were having marital problems; that I was not leaving and his house was safe. I assured him, I would continue to be a good tenant as I had been for the past years. After he calmed down, he expressed regrets that my wife had left me and taken the household goods and our children. Our two wonderful children, Andre' and Felicia were seven and three years old, respectively. The pain of losing my wife was intensified by the thought of losing my children. Those were was the coldest days of my life.

After returning from choir rehearsal that night, I sat down at the card table and wrote my mother-in-law a letter. I told her that Bobbie had left me and had taken the children and household furnishings with her. I told her that I did not know where she was going but I believed she would contact her. I enclosed a check made payable to Bobbie to assist her in establishing herself. After about two months, I got a call from Bobbie. She was in Atlanta, Georgia. Later that year, she said she wanted to come back home. I sent for her and the children. We were happy again for a while. We tried to make up but we could not regain that lovely feeling and could not see eye to eye about our future. About a year later, Bobbie left again. We communicated sparingly. I told her I wanted her back but I could not continue to bear the estrangement. I told her that if she did not come home within twelve months, I would conclude that she did not want to be my wife. One year passed. She did not return and I filed for divorce in 1975. She won custody of our children and I had visitation rights. She moved to Silver Spring, Maryland. I remained in Washington, D.C. I picked up the pieces and got on with my life. I said to myself, this is it for marriage. I vowed to never get married again.

Ms.L.I.: Highly intelligent, voluptuous, and easy to love. I happened to see her at lunch walk across the patio where I worked. She and a friend were sitting on a bench eating a tuna sandwich. There was something about her demeanor and body that drew me to her. I walked up to her and asked if she worked for the agency. She replied, yes. I introduced myself and told her that I worked for the agency also. I asked her for her office phone number. I called her that afternoon and offered her a ride home. As we talked, I could tell right away that we were intellectually compatible. She was easy to talk to, a natural beauty and very smart. She had relationship problems in the past and was reluctant to enter into a relationship with me. It did not take long to change her mind. I would take her to lunch several times a week. We became lovers. She was good at the art of making love. She would not complain when I had to leave her and attend to my business. We were tight for several years and had a lot of fun. We never talked marriage and slowly we drifted apart. She found another friend and eventually got married.

Ms. F. T.: I had a very dear male friend named Bud Montague (mentioned earlier). He owned an auto repair shop. Now, I have always been interested in automobiles. So, I would volunteer to help him on weekends and some evenings when I had time. One weekend, he told me his girlfriend, whom I had met, had a friend that sometimes accompanied them on trips to New York.

He invited me to accompany them on their next trip so I could meet his girlfriend's friend. He had described her as well built and friendly. He wondered why she did not have a boyfriend. I was happy to accept the invitation. The very next weekend, we got together. She was chocolate brown, attractive and reserved. I later learned that she did not live in Washington, D.C. Rather, she lived in Culpepper, Virginia about 50 miles from Washington. I would always meet her in Washington when she came up to visit Bud and his girlfriend. We would go out and have fun. She loved dancing and the blues. She had a mean streak in her personality and was conservative with her love. But when she was in the mood, she was very good. Our courtship, though exciting, did not last too long. My friend, Bud died. His garage closed. I lost track of his girlfriend because I never knew where she lived. I did not get my girlfriend's phone number or visit her in Culpepper. So, after Bud's death our courtship ended. God bless her. I hope she is well.

Ms. W. Y.: Quiet, unassuming, and blessed with a heavenly body. We met at a low point in my life. I was still healing from my divorce. I found out later that she, too, was a divorcee and like me had vowed never to marry again. Her job would sometimes send her away on travel. I would visit her while she was there and we would have fun. She was well established and independent. She was, and I guess still is, an angel. We had a long solid relationship. Although she was quiet and reserved, she was a terror on the dance floor. Our relationship was unique in that we never had an argument or passed a harsh word between us. During the deepest part of our relationship, I could feel my mind slowly changing about marriage. However, she was firm in her decision not to ever marry again. Our relationship slowly cooled. We finally parted with mutual understanding and respect for one another. Somewhere out there, I know she is the darling I knew and most worthy to share her love with the lucky man in her life. God bless her wherever she is.

Five years after my divorce, I met and married a petite, attractive extrovert named Barbara. I don't know how my first wife and second wife got similar names (my first wife's name was Bobbie). Although their names are similar, their personalities are opposites. I made the mistake of calling Barbara, Bobbie, early in our marriage. She promptly straightened me out with saucy language and I never made that mistake again. Someone said, you learn as much from your failures as you do from your successes. I say, you learn more from your failures. In your successes, your mind, heart and strength are tested. In your failures, your mind, heart, strength and soul are tested. How you handle failure really tells you what you are made of. You can't know how hard it is to get up until you have fallen down. If you are wise, you are stronger when you get up and you are less likely to make the same mistake again.

When we met, I was not thinking of marriage. I had picked up the pieces from my first marriage, I was well into my career as a research scientist, I had bought the house that I was renting from Mr. O'Brien and had started my own landscaping business. However, within six months of our courtship, I discovered deep down within myself a disconnect from real happiness and fulfillment. I began to realize, it is not good for a man to be alone. You could say serendipity brought us together. You see, my former voice instructor, Ms. Janet Helms was telling Barbara about some of her former students (Ms.

Chinaberry Hill

Helms loved to talk about life and relationships during her instruction). Somehow, she began describing me to Barbara. She told Barbara she would like for her to meet me and gave her my office phone number.

One evening as I was posting my ledger, the phone rang. I answered in the customary manner, "Duffy's Landscape Service, may I help you?"

A very sweet and girlish voice said, "Hello, I am interested in some landscape work."

I said, "May I have your name and address?"

She said, "My name is Barbara and I live at number 10 Cedar Street, N.W."

"Very good," I said. "That is not too far from my office." As we talked I realized that number 10 Cedar Street, N.W. was an apartment house. I thought she may have been the owner although she sounded rather young. As we continued to talk, I sensed she was as interested in the landscaper as the landscape. I asked for her phone number and followed up with a call the next evening.

Her daughter answered and said, "Mama is out of town. I will tell her you called when she returns." This went on for several months. I became very interested in meeting this woman. I did not ask her where she worked. I began to think, this lady must be a traveling salesperson or had a government job that required a lot of travel. So I finally gave up on calling her via phone. I had experiments going on in the laboratory in Beltsville. On my way to Beltsville from my office I passed within a block of her address. My experiments required me to visit the laboratory many times on weekends.

On my way to the laboratory, I would stop by the apartment house and call for Barbara. Her beautiful and pregnant daughter would come to the door and say "Mama is out of town but I will tell her you called when she returns." This went on for several weekends. I am now thinking, is this woman a movie star, diplomat or what? Her elusive behavior kindled my desire to meet her. So, I said to myself, I will try one more time and if I fail to find her, I will give up and conclude it was not meant for us to meet. The next Sunday, I had to go to the laboratory to observe one of my experiments. I stopped at 10 Cedar Street, N.W. took a deep breath and knocked at the door.

Lo and behold, a petite, brown-skinned, very attractive lady answered the door and said, "Hello. Would you come in?"

I said, "No, sorry I am on my way to the laboratory to check on an experiment."

We chatted briefly. I reached out my hand as if I was going to shake hers but instead, I kissed her. She was most surprised and before she could recover, I said bye and left.

We talked via phone for several weeks before her schedule allowed us to get together. I remember our first date was at the Arena Stage Theater in downtown D.C. It was a live play. I don't remember the title but it was not very good and Barbara had difficulty staying awake.

After nodding off several times, she finally asked if she could lay her head on my shoulder. I replied, of course. The play was dull and I was happy that she felt comfortable enough with me to rest her head on my shoulder on our first date. Before long, we settled into a serious relationship. We both had been married before and had children. We both loved music and were singers. Barbara had a girlfriend named Joan Warren. The two were like twins. Most of the time, they would be together. In fact they were so close, I wondered how I was going to get time alone with Barbara. I later learned Barbara was a hard-working woman. She was working two jobs so her social life was limited. Working long hours also accounted for her being tired and sleepy a lot.

I was working full-time for the federal government and running my landscape business. So, my social life was also limited. This facilitated our relationship. We quickly became best friends and shortly thereafter, lovers. I was very happy with our relationship but had not thought seriously about marriage. We would go out together on weekends as often as our schedules would allow. I found myself gradually changing my mind about marriage and before the year was gone, I began to look at engagement rings. I did not tell her of my plans or how deeply I had fallen in love with her. I began to see in her everything I needed to fulfill my life.

MY STINT WITH UNCLE SAM

At age 18, we all had to register for the (draft) military service. I graduated in May 1953 having already registered for military service in Augusta. In a couple of weeks, I left Augusta to work on campus (AM&N College, now the University of Arkansas at Pine Bluff), in order to earn enough money to register for the fall semester in September. The United States was at war with Korea at the time. Many of my friends who did not go to college were drafted into the infantry shortly after graduation. If I had not entered college, I, like them, would have been drafted into the military service. Fortunately, Uncle Sam had a college deferment program which allowed you to finish college and then join the military service.

I had not given much thought about serving in the military service. I had thought about it enough to know that it was not the kind of life for me. I had fundamental problems about serving in the military. I asked myself, why I should defend a country that reeked with racial prejudice, segregation, Jim Crowism and contempt for black people. How could I defend a country that enslaved and slaughtered my people by the thousands? How could I serve in the military when the very freedom I was fighting for overseas would be denied me once I returned home? Well by the time I finished college, I had decided to serve my time in the military. I had come up with a rationale that allowed me to be mentally at peace when I took the oath which stated, "I am an American fighting man. I serve in the forces that preserve and protect our way of life and I am willing to give my live in their defense." I said silently to myself after I took the oath. "I do not fight for what my country is today, but for the hope of what my country will be in the future. For by its constitution and its form of government, one day it will, by necessity, grant to all of its citizens the blessings of freedom, liberty and justice regardless of race creed or color."

Upon graduation from college, I went to Saint Louis, Missouri to live with my Aunt Clytis Mae and her husband Uncle Bill. I immediately transferred my military draft board to Saint Louis. I knew I would soon be called to military service. So before I received my draft notice, I visited an army recruiting office. I discussed my situation with the recruiting officer. I told him I knew that if I waited to be drafted, I would go directly into the infantry.

He said, "That's right." I told him with my college training, I felt that I could serve better in another capacity.

He said "You are correct but in order to choose your area of service, you must serve for three years instead of two." I thought about it a while and finally agreed to serve the extra year.

He gave me a series of tests. I scored high in mechanics and intelligence. I opted for the intelligence area. I entered the military in August 1957 in Saint Louis, Missouri. I completed my basic training at Fort Leonard Wood, aka Little Korea. I breezed through basic training and made expert rifleman in my company. After basic training, I was shipped to Ayer, Massachusetts for six months training to become an Electronics Intercept Operator for the Army Security Agency. We were sent from Saint Louis to Massachusetts by train. It was a very enjoyable trip. It was the first time I had taken an overnight trip by train. We had a sleeper and dining car. We arrived in Massachusetts in November. I remember the weather shock. It was 60+ degrees when we left Saint Louis. When we got off the train in Massachusetts, the temperature was in the low 20s. I knew then that I was in for a new weather as well as a new military experience. During that winter, the temperature at times fell to 13 below zero and snow sometimes

Chinaberry Hill

accumulated to five feet. My job with the military required a Top Secret Clearance (TSC). This required a background investigation by the FBI. This background investigation was conducted while I was in training. I had no idea what such an investigation entailed. However, the training officer told us that with the Top Secret Clearance, the army would know more about you than you know about yourself. Also that I would be handling sensitive information vital to the security of the United States and if I violated the TSC, I would be fined $10,000 and sentenced to ten years in prison. In addition, I would be restricted to the United States for ten years after my discharge from military service. While I was in training, the FBI paid a visit to my parents in Augusta. Now, to see FBI Agents in Augusta is very rare. My parents were very concerned. They thought I had gotten in some kind of trouble. After my parents calmed down, the agent assured them that I was in no trouble and their visit was part of a background check for a TSC. I did not know they had visited my home until I had completed my training and was on leave prior to my deployment overseas. My parents asked me why I didn't tell them the FBI would be visiting them. I apologized for putting them under such stress but told them that I had no idea that they would come to our home as a part of the investigation.

Compared to college work, my military training was easy. We used a machine called a "mill." It looked like a typewriter but it had two extra rows of keys. The hardest part for me was to get up to the minimum speed which was 35 words per minute. You see, typewriters were not common in homes or schools in Augusta, except in secretary's office. I had no typing skills at all. Therefore, I worked hard to reach the 35 word per minute minimum speed. After finishing my training, I was given two weeks of leave before my deployment overseas. I headed straight to Saint Louis to see my girlfriend. After spending a few days with my girlfriend and relatives in Saint Louis, I headed to Augusta to see my family and friends. We were allowed to wear our class "A" uniform while on leave. My family was excited to see me in uniform. I was at the peak of fitness sporting my class "A" uniform and army patch. My siblings had many questions about the army. I had to limit what I told them to my basic training. I could not tell them anything about my job. When they found out I worked with secret stuff, they thought I was a spy.

My leave time passed fast and before long I was headed to Seattle, Washington where the USS Mann was waiting to transport me to Okinawa. I arrived in Seattle the day before departure. I went out to take a look at the ship. The USS Mann is a big ship; a twin stacker and longer than a football field. I had purchased a little Brownie Hawkeye Camera. I managed to back away for enough to get a full length picture of the ship but it come out so small until a lot of the detail was missing.

We sailed from Seattle in the early afternoon the following day. The USS Mann was a military charter ship. It carried both civilian and military personnel. Upon boarding, you gave your orders to the receiving sergeant and he assigned you to your quarters. He also placed your name on the duty roster for details you would be pulling while in route. The first day out was almost like a vacation cruise. There was a movie and a recreation room on the top deck. I chose to go up and watch a movie that evening. I remember Charleston Heston was starring in the Ten Commandments. I had not seen this movie, so I was glad to have the opportunity to see it free. I enjoyed it very much. I stayed up on the top deck for a while after the movie relaxing in the cool night breeze and the smooth sailing on the clear calm waters of the Pacific. By the time I got ready to go down to my quarters, I was surprised and dismayed to find that many of my buddies were suffering from sea sickness. Our quarters echoed with the groans of vomiting soldiers and reeked with a most unpleasant odor. So I returned to the upper deck where I spent the rest of the night. Fortunately, I never got sea sick.

Each morning after breakfast, which consisted of generous portions of potatoes, eggs, milk and navy beans, the sergeant would line us up and call out the names of those who had details for that day. The rest of us were free to go back to our quarters or just wander around the ship. Well, three days passed and the sergeant had not called my name. I began to

🍂 Chinaberry Hill 🍂

think something was wrong. Some of my buddies would ask me where I was working. I told them that I had C. Q. Duty (care of quarters). After four days passed and I had not been given a detail, I concluded that my name had been inadvertently left off the duty roster. Because there were about 2,000 aboard ship and about half were civilians. I figured I could, with a little bit of luck, travel the 17 day journey without doing any work. So I decided to play the game to the fullest. Every morning, I would get up and dress with the rest of my buddies. Just before the line-up for details, I would position myself near the back of the pack and when the last name for details was called, I would quickly go up to the upper deck where the civilians hung out. You see, we did not have to wear our fatigues unless we were on detail (working). So I would mix with the civilians until the evening meal when all details ended. Pretty soon, some of my buddies became suspicious but I assured them I had been assigned a detail away and different from their's, One of the major details was scaling (scraping) old paint and applying new paint to the decks and inner hull of the ship. By the time we reached Okinawa, all decks and inner parts of the ship had been freshly painted. My game plan worked. The 17 day trip to Okinawa was like a vacation to me. I did not pull a single detail and I did not tell my buddies of my good fortune until we reached our base in Okinawa.

We stopped overnight in Inchun, Korea to take on some soldiers who were being transferred to Okinawa. Upon departure from Inchun, a ship docked next to our ship, headed back to the United States. We all were standing on the upper deck waving at our buddies who had finished their tour of duty in Korea.

To my surprise, I saw one of my college friends. He recognized me and yelled out to me, "you lucky dog, Korea is hell."

I gave him a go to hell wave without comment. Little did he know, I was not going to Korea but to Okinawa. Two days later, our ship docked in Okinawa. I was struck by the beauty of the island but amazed that there were no trees. I later learned all of the trees had been destroyed by military artillery fire from the big guns of World War II.

Spencer L. Duffy

I was in Okinawa four months before I was deployed to Taiwan, my permanent duty station. On Friday, April 13th, I took my first airplane flight from Okinawa to Taiwan. The aircraft was a twin engine D. C. 3 (known to G.I.'s as the goonie bird). There were no seats on the plane. Rather, a narrow bench ran along each side the entire length of the fuselage. We piled in with full field pack and rifles. The goonie bird roared down the runway and we were off to Taiwan. I sat just behind the starboard wing. The engines were so noisy until conversation was impossible. We occasionally used hand signals to communicate. I was surprised at the bumpy ride. This being my first flight, I thought airplanes rode like they looked as I watched them from the ground. To me, they looked like they were moving effortless through the air as smooth as silk. Boy, was I wrong. The goonie bird rode like a bronco. I was glad when we touched down at the airport in Taipei, the capital city of Taiwan. We debarked with haste. An army truck (6-by) was waiting. It took us up a serpentine rocky mountain road to our duty station about 17 miles outside of Taipei. The compound where I worked was mostly underground with only one entrance and no windows. It operated 24-7. Our duty schedules shifted from the day shift to the evening (swing) shift and finally to the night (midnight to 8:00 am) shift. After a complete rotation, we would get three days off. When we were off duty, we could stay on base or take a truck down the mountain to Taipei. I did not like the rough truck ride down the mountain, so most of the time, I stayed on base.

The Taiwanese had an artillery base a few miles from our post. They had a habit of firing mortar shells across our base to targets on the other side. I remember, one day we heard a mortar coming in. It sounded different from the ones we were used to hearing. As it got closer, we could tell it was coming short of its target and headed for our post. We all scrambled for cover. It fell smack dab in the middle of our compound with a thud. Thank God! It was a dud. Our commander had a talk with the Taiwanese commander and artillery firing across our post ceased.

I spent 18 months in Taiwan. I learned a lot about the city. I took a couple of courses at the University of Maryland at Taiwan. I was surprised to know it was there and more surprised to learn that practically all of the students spoke fluent English and most of their text books were in English. The USO operated a hospitality house in downtown Taipei. The hospitality house was a place you could go and read American newpapers or magazines, listen to American music or just relax in its spacious lounge. When I got tired of the city, I would rent a bicycle and ride out into the countryside. The land around Taipei is relatively flat but surrounded by hills and mountains. Rice paddies are everywhere. I remember spending a long weekend in the countryside with a Taiwanese family whose daughter turned out to be my date for the weekend. I rode my bike up to the house. I saw mama san (mother) and papa san (father) in the yard. I stopped and began a conversation with papa san. He spoke very little English and I spoke very little Chinese, so our conversation was strained. Before long, a beautiful young lady emerged from the house and greeted me in perfect English. She was their daughter. She asked me if I wanted to see her place and show me how they lived. I was pleasantly surprised at her friendliness.

So, I said sure, "I am with you."

They lived in a small mud-brick house with a thatch roof. She had her own private room. Mosquitoes were bad. So she had a mosquito bar over her bed. It was the first time I had seen such a thing. I do not remember eating anything while I was there. However, I did drink a kind of liquor made from rice. I did not like it much but out of good manners, I drank enough for a buzz. After a while, the family left us alone. She took me to her room and before long, we were in bed, safe from the mosquitoes but not from each other arms. It was funny, our vigorous love making seemed to disturb the chickens. They seemed to be monitoring our activity and would begin clucking and cackling when we made too much noise. The next morning, I got up and made ready to ride back into town. I thanked mama san and papa san for my keep and gave their daughter $10.00 ($400.00 in Taiwanese money) and carton of Kool cigarettes.

Spencer L. Duffy

Papa san was up feeding the chickens and gathering firewood. I greeted him politely and he responded kindly. His daughter who was now beside me, said something to him in Chinese.

He smiled. She asked me to come back the next time I had leave. I said I would but I never did. Taiwanese women are quaintly beautiful and treat you like a king. In fact, several of my buddies of higher rank rented houses for their social activities while on leave. For a few U. S. dollars, you could rent an upscale house quipped with maid service and as many girlfriends as you wanted. This was heaven for some of us. Some of the guys in my company married Taiwanese women and stayed in Taiwan after their tour of duty ended. In spite of the beauty and quaintness of the Taiwanese women, after a while, I missed the sultry pulchritude and innate beauty of my African American sisters. I also missed the changing of the seasons. Taiwan is subtropical. There is a rainy season called the monsoon. I never saw it rain so hard for so long. We were issued ponchos to keep the rain out but after a while the blowing rain and high humidity together with the interfacing surface water, it mattered not what kind of rain gear you were wearing, you got wet. Then it turned hot. Summer temperatures can get into the triple digits. It never freezes in the winter but gets cool enough for a light jacket. You could see snow on the mountain tops.

I did not think I would miss snow but after about a year, I began longing for the winter and the ethereal beauty of the four seasons.

My tour of duty with Uncle Sam ended in August 1960. I processed out of Taiwan and took a military night flight to Oakland, California. The flight back home was traumatic. The plane developed engine trouble after about an hour and a half out over the deepest and most shark infested area of the Pacific Ocean. I was seated by the window just behind the starboard wing. I noticed some kind of liquid sticking to the glass. At first, I thought it was rain but then I saw that it was brown. I knew then it was oil. The plane began to slow down and tilt to one side.

Chinaberry Hill

The flight engineer came into the passenger compartment, saw the oil which by this time had covered the window. His face was red as a beet. He rushed back to the cockpit.

The intercom crackled. "This is your pilot. We have developed engine trouble and will have to land in Guam."

We had gone too far to turn back to Taiwan. Our flight was scheduled to land in Hawaii. For a few seconds there was a strange silence. Then some of the civilian family members began to scream and cry and say we are going to crash. The flight attendants tried to comfort them. We GIs just sat in silence starring at the oil that was coating the windows. I was not afraid. I was more concerned about fire than crashing into the Pacific. I guess my military training had mentally prepared me for such an event. I could feel the plane losing altitude. I had taken a $100,000 accidental death insurance policy on myself. Mama and Daddy were the beneficiaries. I was cool. I said to myself, well if this is it, at least my family will have means to have a better life for themselves. About an hour and a half later, we limped into Guam. Cheers went up as we touched down at Guam Air Force Base. It was after midnight and except for the runway lights, it was pitch dark. We disembarked from the plane and spent the rest of the night in the airport. The air force mechanics worked on our crippled plane for the rest of the night. The next morning, we re-boarded the same plane. Some of the civilian passengers were reluctant to re-board. The flight crew assured us that the plane was repaired and air worthy. We took off to Hawaii. This time we had no trouble. Thanks to the excellent air force mechanics, they got it right. Our 10 hour flight to Hawaii was smooth. The Pacific looked like a blue blanket spread beneath us and the sky a blue ceiling suspended above us. It was a perfect day for flying. We landed in Hawaii in the early evening. We had a three hour layover. I stayed in the airport but I got a glimpse of the sheer beauty of the island and its people. We re-boarded and took off to Oakland Air Force Base in Oakland, California. A feeling of relief, accomplishment and thankfulness rushed over me as we touched down. I had about a month left on my tour of duty.

Spencer L. Duffy

Because of my agricultural science background, I was assigned to the pest control unit at the air force base. My job was to inspect military dependents housing, treat for any insect or rodent infestation and control the gopher population which constantly made unsightly mounds on the lawns. We used powered cyanide to kill them in their burrows. Now cyanide is a potent and deadly poison. A few whiffs of the stuff can be fatal. I wore a field grade military gas mask when applying cyanide. There were strict rules for accounting for, handling and storing cyanide. Any violation resulted in a court martial. I was very careful and had no trouble with residents who had unusual pest infestations. For the most part, I was my own boss after I reported for duty and got my assignment.

The last week of duty was spent processing out. I turned in all of my military gear except my class A uniform which I was allowed to keep. The staff sergeant asked me if I wanted to re-up and consider a career in the military. I replied without hesitation, "No sir." He then began to exclaim the benefits of a military career and said I would get an automatic promotion if I would re-up. He could tell from my expression that I was not impressed.

Finally, he asked me, "What do you want out of the military?"

I quickly replied, "Me."

My last day in the military finally came in late August 1960. I was given my good conduct metal, my honorable discharge papers and my Form DD-214. I walked out of Oakland Air Force Base a free man. Once Uncle Sam releases you, he is through with you. I thought at least he would give me a military ride to the Greyhound Bus station. Well, I caught a cab to the bus station and headed across country to Saint Louis, Missouri. Trailways, Greyhound's competitor, seemed to take longer for long trips because it stopped at many small towns and villages that Greyhound just passed through. In fact, as a boy, I wanted to be a bus driver, although I noticed there were no Greyhound or Trailways drivers that looked like me. I later found out that neither company hired African Americans as bus drivers. What's more, they did not particularly want us to ride the bus except when we sat behind the white passengers.

Chinaberry Hill

While in college, I got put off of the Greyhound several times for refusing to give up my seat to a white passenger.

My trip via Greyhound from Oakland, California to Saint Louis, Missouri was exciting. My bus was a double decker express. (That model is no longer made). It was the most comfortable bus Greyhound had made. I chose to ride in the upper level just behind the windshield. You could prop your feet upon the dash board and between the windshield and the sky lights in the roof, you had a good view of the country side. It took a day and a half to go from Oakland to Saint Louis. We made about four scheduled stops between Oakland and Saint Louis. We would have a couple of rest stops during the day and a stop for dinner in the evening. After which the bus would run non-stop all night. I remember two stops were in Texas. Now, I had always heard that everything was big in Texas. Well, I don't know about that but I am a witness that the state of Texas is big. We entered Texas a little before dark one evening. We rode all night and when we stopped for breakfast the next morning, we were still in Texas.

Upon returning to Saint Louis, I stayed with my Aunt Clytis Mae and Uncle Bill. Grand Pop was staying with them at that time. I bought a 1954 Ford two-door sedan (six years old). I paid cash for it from mustering out money I got from Uncle Sam. Before long, I found work as a grounds keeper at a private up-scale high school (The Principia). John Glen's (the astronaut) daughter was a student at that time. The Principia was located on an expansive campus in Clayton, a surburb of Saint Louis. I worked at the Principia until I left Saint Louis. During my stay in Saint Louis, I enjoyed helping my Aunt Mae and Uncle Bill around the house and talking with Grand Pop Henry. He would draw me into intellectual conversations about history and current events. I marveled at his intelligence and memory. He was in his 90's and growing physically feeble, but his mental sharpness was phenomenal. Uncle Bill was a quiet man. He knew Saint Louis like the palm of his hand. He was a walking atlas. My Aunt Mae, as we affectionately called her, was a lay minister. She would frequently hold religious services in her apartment. By my working, I missed a lot of them. However, Grand Pop would fill me in when I got home.

Before long, I found a girlfriend and was out a lot dating. Aunt Mae would not go to sleep until I got home, albeit sometimes very late. I would strive to get home before midnight which she suggested but frequently failed. Saint Louis was a rough city. Aunt Mae's son, Charles had been beaten up by a gang a few years earlier and was hospitalized for a long time. My being young and just out of the military, I think she feared for my safety although she never openly expressed it. As for me, I was fearless. I had just gotten out of the army and I felt I could handle the jitter bugs in Saint Louis. When I would come in very late, I would park my car in the back of the apartment besides the alley. I would sneak in through the back door. It never failed.

Just as I entered the hallway which led to my bedroom, Aunt Mae would say, "Good morning Spencer."

I would sheepishly reply, "Good morning Aunt Mae."

My other aunt, Aunt Armentha lived around the corner from Aunt Mae. She had an efficiency which she shared with her beautiful teenage daughter, Anna Louise. Aunt Armentha was a serious Sunday School Teacher and Bible scholar. I liked talking to her about religious matters and Biblical questions. Her daughter (my cousin) Anna Louise loved to hang out with me. We would occasionally go out to dinner. At that time, it was customary to leave a tip for the waitress or waiter upon departing the restaurant. I noticed Louise would always lag behind me as we left the restaurant. After a while, I realized that she was collecting the tip that I had left for the waiter. I think she knew better but was showing her dissatisfaction with the service or was pulling a prank. I had a hard time convincing her that waiters and waitresses depended on tips to make up for their very low wages. I finally convinced her to leave the tips. But to make sure, I sometimes would put Louise in front of me as we left the restaurant. Anna Louise wanted to go everywhere with me. She could not understand why I did not take her with me when I went out on dates with my girlfriend. If she knew I was going out on a date, she would get in my car and wait for me to come out. I would sometimes have to physically remove her from the car before I could leave to pick up my girlfriend.

Aunt Armentha's efficiency was getting too small for her and her teenage daughter. So I convinced her to share a larger apartment with me. We found a large two bedroom apartment down the street from Aunt Mae's apartment. It was a second floor apartment with large rooms and a long hall way. It was a good arrangement. For the next two years which was the balance of my stay in Saint Louis, we enjoyed our new dwelling place. We all shared in keeping the place clean and comfortable. It was Louise's job to keep the living room clean and to sweep the carpeted stairwell daily. Now Aunt Armentha did not like to cook, in fact Aunt Clytis Mae told me when we got the apartment together that I would end up cooking for myself. I made a deal with Aunt Armentha. I told her I would pay half of the rent, buy the groceries and the coal for the furnace (the apartment was heated by a coal furnace), and keep the apartment warm if she would prepare one meal (dinner) a day, Monday through Friday. (Most of the times I would eat out with my girlfriend on weekends). That worked out just fine. I quickly learned to stock the furnace when I left for work and adjust the damper so that it would keep the apartment warm all day. Anna Louise was off to school and Aunt Armentha and I were off to work. Louise was the first to get home. I would arrive later and Aunt Armentha was last to get home. However, without complaining she always fixed us a nice dinner.

My time in Saint Louis was enjoyable and enlightening. My being from a small town (Augusta), Saint Louis exposed me to city life. I had fun learning the city and dating the girls. I was aware of the dangers of the city and always careful to pick my friends and the places I went to socialize. I remember, my girlfriend and I went to a new club one Friday evening. It was an okay place but I had an uncomfortable feeling after we had been there for a little while. She was really enjoying herself. I told her I did not feel good about the place. She asked me why.

I said, "I don't know." I said, "I think it's time for us to go." She reluctantly followed me as I prepared to leave the joint. Just as we left, fighting broke out. As we walked to my car, shooting started and as we stepped off the sidewalk, someone tried to run us down with his car. We got away unharmed. She was amazed at my perception. She kept asking me how did I know something was wrong. I told her I seemed to have a sixth sense about danger and that was not the first time I followed my ESP and escaped from harm's way. The newspaper the next day reported the incident and revealed one person was killed and several persons injured that night.

I later joined Saint Peters AME Church where Aunt Armentha and Louise were members. Aunt Armentha taught the adult Sunday School class. I learned a lot about the Bible and Christianity while in her class. I sang in the church choir and rendered my first solo ("His Eye Is On the Sparrow") under the very capable direction of Mrs. Fisher. I accidentally ran upon a girlfriend whom I knew from visiting various schools in Arkansas. She became my best girlfriend while in Saint Louis. We remained very close friends after I left Saint Louis and until she finally got married.

After two years in Saint Louis, I decided that I wanted a graduate degree from Howard University in Washington, D.C. I told Aunt Armentha that winter that I was going to leave the coming summer. Aunt Armentha understood, wished me well and assured me that she and Louise could handle the apartment. So, in late June that next summer, I said goodbye to Aunt Armentha, my cousin Louise, my girlfriend and the rest of my Saint Louis family. I packed my few belongings in my car and headed out to Washington, D.C. Now at that time, Interstate 70 or 81 did not exist. The route to Washington, D.C. from Saint Louis was Highway 50 East all the way. I left Saint Louis around 9 am. I drove all day and all night. I only stopped for gas (I used the restroom when I stopped for gas). Aunt Armentha had prepared enough food for the journey. So I had no need to stop at a restaurant. I had serviced my car very well and was sure it would make the 1,000 mile trip. However, I had one concern. I had one bad tire and my spare though fully inflated was bald. At that time cars had tube-type tires. My front right tire had a blister on the sidewall which meant that the sidewall was weak at that point and subject to blow out. Well, at that time, we used tires until they were bald as humpty dumpty. Fortunately, the tire manufacturers provided a patch called a boot. This was a heavy piece of rubber that could be placed inside the tire at the weak spot. It was glued in place between the tube and the inside of the tire. This reinforced that weak spot in the tire and greatly reduced the chances of a blowout. I did not have AAA or any roadside emergency road service. So I took off on faith. Well, I did fine. I had no trouble at all except at about 3 am on a foggy morning in the state of Virginia, I had a close encounter with an oil tanker tractor trailer. You see, 50 at that time was a hilly, two lane serpentine highway. As I came around a curve at the top of the hill, in a pea soup fog, a fully loaded oil tanker was barreling down on me at excessive speed. To make bad matters worse, he was in the middle of the road. I guess he could not see me or the center line on the road. I hit the shoulder to avoid hitting him head on. Fortunately, the shoulder was solid enough and the ditch was shallow. The truck driver knew he had run me off the road. He slowed down as if he was going to stop but didn't. I coasted to a stop and got out to see if my rear tires were on solid ground so I could pull back upon the highway. The right rear tie had cut a deep rut in the shoulder on the edge of the ditch. Now my left rear tire was on the edge of the pavement. So my car is not completely off the road. I had to think quickly because another vehicle coming in the same direction in this pea soup fog would surely hit me. So I jumped in my car, put in it second gear, gave it a goose of gas and slowly let out on the clutch. I could feel the right rear wheel pulling but beginning to spin. I eased up off the gas a little and it caught hold to enough solid ground to ease me back upon the highway. Just as I got back upon the highway, another tractor trailer came barreling up behind me. I put the petal to the metal and gained enough speed to avoid being hit in the rear. He passed me running like a bat out of hades. I breathed a sign and said a little prayer as I watched his tail lights disappear in the fog.

Spencer L. Duffy

Well, I arrived in Washington, D.C. mid afternoon. It was a sunny day and I was tired from the 24 hour drive. However, I got excited when I approached the Memorial Bridge. I could see the Washington Monument, the low profile of the city, the unfettered mall from the Lincoln Monument all the way to the Capital. I said to myself, "Oh what a beautiful city," (unlike Saint Louis which was smoky, dirty and sprawling). Washington was clear, compact and clean. I liked the city at first sight.

I came in on Constitution Avenue, turned left on 13th Street and stopped at the first hotel I saw—The Whitlaw. At first glance, I could tell it was not a four star facility. However, I was tired and wanted a place to rest. So I pulled up, parked in front on the street and went in. When I entered the lobby, I could tell it was not a quality facility. In fact, it was a step above a flop house. It was a hang-out for prostitutes, gamblers and others whose character left much to be desired. Well, I was tired and just wanted a room in which to sleep. So I checked in. My room was on the second floor. Surprisingly, it was clean but the lock had taken a beating as if someone had tried to break in. The bed was not much more than a cot that stood independently over against the wall. It was clean and had two white sheets and a light blanket for cover. Well, I considered after living in Saint Louis for two years, I could live at the Whitlaw for one night. So I pulled the bed from the other side of the room and positioned it squarely across the door. I washed my face and hands and settled in for the night. It was relatively quiet except for an occasional outburst from someone arguing in the lobby. In a few minutes, I was fast asleep. When I awoke, the sun was shining through my window. I got up, cleaned up and went out for breakfast. I found a little restaurant on T Street. I can't recall the name but the food was very good, reasonably priced and the waitress was friendly and good looking. So, I was off to a good start. I picked up a morning paper called the *Washington News* on my way back to the hotel. Back in my room, I glanced at the headlines and quickly turned to the add section. By checkout time (12:00 noon), I had found me a room on 14th Street about a mile from the Whitlaw. I checked out of the Whitlaw and headed to my new residence. It was a nice little room on the third floor of an apartment building owned and operated by a relatively young and attractive lady. I was pleased and impressed by the caliber of people I met in Washington. I stayed there until I got a job at E. H. Bauer Landscape Company based in Kensington, Maryland. I later moved to a room in a private home in the 1300 block of Irving Street N.W. This was a private home, owned by Mrs. Cooper, a retired government employee. She was full figured, friendly lady who only rented to men. I thought that was strange. So one day I asked her why she rented only to men. She said women were more difficult to get along with and frequently they would bring men in to stay overnight. This, Mrs. Cooper did not allow. Furthermore, she told me to my surprise, that men kept their room cleaner than women. Mrs. Cooper laid down the rules of the house to me. She knew I was single and new to the city. She told me when I found a girlfriend, she wanted to meet her and talk with her. She said, your girlfriend can visit you but cannot stay in your room overnight. That was fine with me because all of my girlfriends in Saint Louis had their own apartments and seldom did I stay overnight with them. If we had a heavy date, we would go to a hotel or motel. So Mrs. Cooper and I got along just fine. I stayed with her until I registered for the fall semester at Howard University Graduate School. After registration, (by this time I am married) I found an apartment in the 2700 block of Georgia Avenue near the campus. I enrolled in the Science Department the fall semester of 1963. I wanted a graduate degree in a field close to my undergraduate degree which was in technical agriculture (This degree was different from the traditional vocational agriculture degree which included a teaching component). So Botany at Howard was the logical choice.

 My experience at Howard was very enlightening and rewarding. I liked the campus layout, the depth of instruction and the status of the university. Howard was (and probably still is) known as the Capstone of higher education among the Historically Black Colleges and Universities in America. I was excited and eager to get on with my studies. I took a major in Plant Science that lead to a Masters degree in Botany

Spencer L. Duffy

with a specialty in Plant Physiology. As in my undergraduate studies, I worked part time while in Graduate School. This was necessary to pay my way and to support my family. I worked evenings and weekends at Nero's Service station on the corner of Georgia Avenue and Park Road N.W. Now, I have always been interested in mechanics. So I enjoyed learning and working as a station attendant. Mr. Nero was a good business man. He saw my interest in mechanics. So he would allow me to assist the mechanic, Mr. Montague, when I was not busy on the line. Mr. Montague and I became very good friends. In fact, he became the only male friend I had while at Howard. Mr. Montague was ambitious. He had his own small shop on V street N. W. Where he worked weekends and holidays. I learned a lot about cars while working with Mr. Montague and I was heartily sorry when he passed suddenly from a massive heart attack.

After graduation from Howard University, I applied for a position as a plant scientist at the National Arboretum, the National Botanical Gardens and the United States Department of Agriculture (USDA). Six months later, I was hired as a Plant Physiologist (I believe the first African American) with the Agricultural Research Service USDA. I worked in the pesticides Regulations Laboratory in Beltsville, Maryland for 15 years. I became a journeyman research scientist and published several scientific articles on plant physiology. My colleagues were graduates of Auburn University, George Washington University and The University of Maryland. They accepted me as a fellow professional but viewed my skills and abilities with some skepticism. I was very confident of my skills and the excellence of my instructors at Howard University. So I enjoyed the challenge. We worked mostly independently on various research projects relative to the effects of pesticides on plants. If our findings were good enough, they were would be published in various journals of plant science. I remember one project required applying accurately small quantities (as little as one milliliter) of liquid to a surface. We searched the universe of scientific equipment and found no such device. So I asked my colleague, Bernard Schneider if he would join me infabricating such a device. He agreed. Within six months, we had come up with a hand held, battery operated multi-volume sprayer that could accurately apply one to 1000 ml of liquid to a given surface. Our findings were published later that year. Now, had we been in private industry (all research at that time became property of the federal government and could not be patented to an individual) this fabrication could have easily been patented. In fact, a company after reviewing our articles manufactured a carbon copy of our sprayer for applying pesticides to garden plants. As of this writing, this sprayer is still on the market.

My research career was cut short by the advent of the de-regulation policies of the Reagan Administration. Consequently, the Pesticide Relations Laboratory in Beltsville was closed and I was, with great anguish, involuntarily transferred to Headquarters Environmental Protection Agency in Washington, D.C. (My duty station was in Crystal City, Arlington, Virginia). I vigorously fought the transfer. I pressed management hard to find a laboratory somewhere in the federal government that would allow me to continue as a research plant scientist. Management finally came up with an offer in a laboratory in Gulfport, Mississippi. Now, my being form Arkansas which is next door to Mississippi and having heard Nina Simone sing her hit tune, "Mississippi G.D." I refused the offer. So, this was the end of my research career. I spent the last 10 years of my career with the federal government leading teams of scientists in the production of federal regulations regarding the effectiveness and safety of pesticides. Our work appeared routinely in the Federal Register.

The last 10 years of my career were difficult for me because I felt Uncle Sam had betrayed me. I did not spend four years studying science as an undergraduate and two more years as a graduate student only to end up doing paper work at headquarters EPA. Thanks to my first Supervisor Ms. Juanita Wills and her secretary Ms. Delores Henderson (affectionately called "Dee") who gave me good counsel during my transition. They are my friends and are most worthy of my enduring appreciation and respect.

Three years after being transferred to Headquarters EPA, I decided to open my own landscaping business. Because the work at headquarters was less difficult and demanding than the work in the laboratory, I felt I could run a part-time landscaping business evenings and weekends. My agricultural background and my work with landscaping companies while in college gave me a good technical background for the landscaping business. However, I felt I needed some business training to be a successful entrepreneur. So I enrolled in Howard University's evening small business class. After finishing that course which was very enlightening, I took a course in Landscape Architecture at the USDA's Graduate School in Washington D. C. Then I applied for a Small Business Loan from the Small Business Administration to purchase a truck and tools. My application was rejected. So, I decided to finance my landscaping business myself out of our personal savings, much to the consternation of my wife. I told her I would put back the money I took from our savings account from earnings from my landscaping business within three years. This I did. Duffy's Landscape Service thrived and became a major source of income for my family. In fact, Duffy's Landscape Service practically paid for our daughter Felicia's education at The University of Maryland. When our son Andre' got old enough, he became my main assistant. I hired an older young man named Lawrence Parker whom I met through his mother Ms. Catherine. She saw me parked on the street near her apartment and asked if I would move some furniture for her. Now, my truck was empty at the time so, I agreed. She said she had a son Lawrence, who would help me. Lawrence was three years older then my son and appeared eager to work. So, after I moved the furniture for Ms. Catherine, I asked Lawrence if he would help me with my landscaping business evening and on weekends. He agreed and became a good and reliable employee. I opened my office at 9th and Kennedy Streets, N.W. in 1973. Here, I would receive and counsel customers, do paperwork and take orders for future jobs. Duffy's Landscape Service was a well-run and well respected business. It provided expert landscape construction for new homes as well as established dwelling throughout the Washington Metropolitan area. It never ran ads but relied on word of mouth for perpetuating its customer base. Duffy's Landscape Service closed in 1993 after 25 years of fulfilling its mission, "making more livable our natural environment." I had hoped to turn the business over to my son Andre' or Lawrence but by this time they had their own jobs and showed no interest in owning a landscape company.

MY SECOND MARRIAGE

When I got married the first time at the tender age of 29 to my college sweetheart whom I had courted many years, no one could have told me that I would be single, divorced and alone again after 10 years of a relatively good marriage. But as the saying goes, "the best laid plans of men and mice do go astray." After divorce from my first wife, Bobbie, I said I would not get married again. I looked at myself and said, "I am all right." I am well situated in my career, I have my own business and I am socially well adjusted and financially secure. So why bother. Well that worked for a while. However, deep within me I felt a disconnect from wholeness and fulfillment. I had bought the house we were renting at the time of my divorce. I discovered I did not like coming home to an empty house and the loneliness that accompanied such an estate. I came to realize what the scriptural statement meant when it said, it is not good for man to be alone. I had no problem meeting and keeping a girlfriend but regardless how good a girlfriend can be there is something about a wife that a girlfriend cannot give regardless how sweet and loving she may be.

One day, my former voice teacher, Mrs. Janet Helms was talking with one of her students. Now Mrs. Helms loved to talk about life and relationships. Somehow she mentioned my name to her and said she thought she should meet me. Now, it had been two years since I studied voice under Mrs. Helms. I had

Chinaberry Hill

no idea that she would remember any of the personal things we talked about or that she had match-making skills.

We courted for about a year. Early on, we seemed to be very comfortable with each other and serious about our relationship. We both loved music were singers and had been married before. She was employed by the Federal Government with the General Services Administration and a student of Music at The University of the District of Columbia. I was employed with the Federal Environmental Protection Agency and owner operator of my part time landscaping business. I later discovered that Barbara was working two jobs when we met which limited her social life and accounted for her being tired and sleepy a lot. Because of my business, my social time was also limited. However, we managed to arrange adequate time to accommodate our courtship.

Barbara had a girlfriend named Joan Warren. These two were like twins. Most of the time, they would be together. They were so close, I sometime wondered if I could get them apart long enough to get the time I needed alone with Barbara. As our relationship grew, we found the time needed to nurture our courtship. Barbara became my steady girlfriend. I was very happy with our relationship but had not seriously considered a second marriage. After about a year into our courtship, I felt myself slipping away from my vow not to get married again. My love for Barbara was very strong and seemed to be getting stronger by the day. I did not tell her how deeply I loved her. I saw in her everything I needed to fulfill my dreams and make my life complete.

Our family reunion was to be held in Los Angeles, California the following year (August 1979). I asked Barbara if she would go with me to the family reunion. She said yes. So, I began planning our trip to Los Angeles and a surprise for her at our talent show during our family reunion. I started looking for an engagement ring. I did not tell Barbara my plans. My brother-in-law who lived in Arkansas, had purchased a motor home. He and his wife (my sister Nancy) and several other family members had planned to drive to Los Angeles via motor home. He asked me if I wanted to come along to help with the driving. Now, Sam knew I had experience in driving large vehicles and was trained in automotive mechanics. I agreed but with one condition. I told Sam I would come along and help him with the driving only if he would permit me to bring my girlfriend. He said, no problem. The motor home was large enough to accommodate 13 passengers.

By this time, I had found the engagement ring. Sam called me and asked about the maintenance he should have done on the motor home before the long trip to Los Angeles. I advised him to have all the drive belts and hoses replaced, and to make sure the tires, lights, battery and windshield wipers were all in good condition. He took my advice. However, when we got to Arkansas, I inspected the motor home just to make sure it was road worthy for such a trip. However, I took my tools along just in case we had trouble on the road.

Sure enough, in Arizona at about 3 am, I heard a loud bang from the engine compartment. The vehicle began shaking violently. Sam was driving. I advised him to slow way down to about 10 miles per hour. He put the hazard lights on and we crept to the next exit which was about a mile away. Fortunately, there was a Chevrolet Dealership on this exit and the motor home was a General Motors product. We pulled in on the well lit parking lot. I got out, raised the hood and saw that the fan belt had been severed by the fan blade which had been broken off due to a lose bolt in the alternator bracket. I also discovered the loose bolt came off because it had been stripped when the mechanic replaced the alternator belt. This bolt accounted for the broken belt fan blade, noise and the vibration. Fortunately, there was no damage to the engine or radiator. By daybreak, I had removed the belt and fan assembly. We waited for the dealership to open. At 7 am the parts department opened. We purchased a belt, fan and fan clutch assembly and an alternator bolt. We had a problem in that the only fan assembly they had was regular duty and the motor home called for a heavy duty fan. Well, I told Sam we had no choice but to install the regular duty fan assembly and hope it would hold up until we got to Los Angeles and would work well enough to keep the vehicle from overheating. Well, it did and we arrived in Los Angeles,

Chinaberry Hill

California without further trouble. In fact we drove back to Arkansas without changing to a heavy duty fan and without further trouble. However, I advised my brother-in-law to have the heavy duty fan put on as soon as possible.

Our family reunion always included a talent show where each family member would make some kind of presentation. So, after I read one of my poems and sang a song, I called Barbara to join me on stage. Again, she was very surprised. I presented her to the family, announced our engagement and presented to her a .5 caret blue diamond engagement ring. While her face was still radiant with joy and surprise, I kissed her and we exited with generous applause.

Barbara and I got married on my birthday, October 25, 1980 at Mount Zion Baptist Church, (her church) at 14th and Gallatin Streets, N.W., Washington, D.C. A songwriter once wrote, "love is better the second time around." Well, I am a living witness that much of the song is true. Barbara and I have been married 30 beautiful years without any serious domestic issues and every now and then she will do something that reminds me that the best is yet to come. She is love personified. Who is she-who snaps my head as she walks by

> *Who is she-who makes me feel like I can fly*
> *Who is she-who makes me think I own the world*
> *My dearest, my darling, my girl*
> *Who is she-who takes me by the hand*
> *Who is she-who leads me to a wonderland*
> *Who is she-who loves me til I sweat*
> *My sweetheart, my lady, my pet*
> *Who is she-whose love will never die*
> *Who is she-who knows but ask not why*
> *Who is she-who rules my fragile life*
> *MY FRIEND, MY LOVER, MY WIFE*

RETIREMENT YEARS

I worked for the federal government 27 years. With my three years service in the army, I accumulated just enough time (30 years) to retire with full benefits. When I was involuntarily transferred out of the laboratory to headquarters I vowed not to work a day beyond 30 years. So, I retired in December 1992 at the age of 58. Frankly, when I began my career with the federal government in 1965, I had planned to retire at age 45. However, someone said, "The best laid plans of men and mice do go astray." I failed to factor in those circumstances and life events that have a way of altering our best made plans. Barbara and I had been married 11 years when I retired. We had planned our retirement future shortly after we got married. She retired several years ahead of me by taking an early out option. At the time she retired, we were building our custom home in Beltsville, Maryland. We moved in our new home in August 1991 but kept our house in Washington, D.C. as rental property. Between our annuities, our rental property and my landscape business, we were able to live comfortably on our retirement income.

From the beginning of my working career, I was determined to retire early while my health was still good and my wife and I could experience a level of freedom and enjoy the fruits of our labor which is impossible during your working years. So far, so good. At this writing, I have been retired 18 years and all I can say is, "How sweet it is."

Chinaberry Hill

In our retirement, Barbara and I remain very active. In fact Barbara has drifted in and out of the workforce as instructor of cosmetology several times since her retirement. We sing in several choirs, go where we want to go and basically do what we want to do. I find it interesting that I have to limit my activities or I will be so busy until I forget that I am retired. In my latter retirement years, I find it quite rewarding to keep up with the grandchildren, maintain our home and cars, visit family and carve out special time for Barbara and me. The most rewarding thing I find in retirement is that you are in complete control of your time. One thing I longed for during my working years and that was to be able to take a nap in the middle of the day. During my college days and on into my working career I would get very sleepy in the early afternoon. Sometimes in college, during my two o'clock classes, I would not get full benefit of the lecture because most of my energy was spent fighting sleep. After I was transferred to EPA Headquarters in 1980, I would get so sleepy after lunch until I would get up from my desk and walk down ten flights of stairs and sometimes all the way to the outside in order to keep from falling asleep at my desk. I said to myself, when I retire, I am going to get up in the middle of the bed, in the middle of the day and take me a mid-day uninterrupted nap. I was pleasantly surprised to learn how refreshing and invigorating a mid-day nap can be. However, I confess, I sometimes get so busy I forget to take my mid-day nap but I always get back to it before long. I think the Mexicans have something good going on in their culture that we Americans should adopt.

Retirement which was once called the golden years is a wonderful time of life. However, to reap its full benefits, you should start planning for your retirement when you start your working career; i.e. your first job. Although the federal government is known to have a good retirement system, I took advantage of all the supplementary programs designed to enhance retirement. I participated fully in the IRA which became available to government workers about 6 years prior to my retirement. I also maximized the TSP (Thrift Savings Plan) when it became available to me. Under the Civil Service

Spencer L. Duffy

Retirement System (CSRS) your unused sick leave was credited to your annuity. Fortunately, I was very healthy during my working years. I had accumulated a little more than one year of sick leave when I retired. Therefore, my annuity is based on 31 years of service although I worked only 30 years (30 years of service and one year of unused sick leave).

I closed my landscaping business one year after retiring from the federal government. Now that I am fully retired, a senior citizen in the autumn of my life, I can truly say that retirement can be the golden years if you adequately prepare for it.

I WILL BUILD ME A HOUSE

As a single man, long before I thought about marriage, I knew the kind of house I wanted. I wanted a custom built rambler with full basement. I looked until I found a company that sold house plans. I found such a company in Pennsylvania. I sent for their catalogue of house plans. It arrived in the mail a few weeks later. From this catalogue, I picked my dream house, ordered the blueprints and carried them around with me for 20 years. When I found a place to build my house, I was engaged to my second wife, Barbara. I showed her the plans and surprisingly, she liked them. Unfortunately, the site I had chosen on which to build turned out to be unsuitable because of soil conditions that resulted in a failed percolation test (passed percolation test was required for building sites outside of the public sewer system). So I began looking for another site in the same area. I found a site about a half mile from the previous one.

This site had public water and sewage. However, I found it was heir property. Four persons were involved and all had to agree before it could be sold. It was a one acre plot on a wooded hillside with and old abandoned house on it. I liked the plot. So I made a down payment with the understanding the owners were working in good faith to agree to sell. Well, it took several years before the heirs agreed to sell. By that time, the price of the property had almost doubled. Well, I liked the lot, so I bought it. I planned to rehabilitate the old house and live in it until I built the new house which was to be placed in front of the old house. However, as my luck runs, 30 days after I purchased the lot the county condemned the old house and give me 30 days to tear it down. I protested bitterly but to no avail.

I happened to know a member of my church who was a remodeling contractor. I told him about my problem and he came out and demolished the old house at a very modest price. Today, I cannot understand why the county would not allow me to rehabilitate the old house. About one year later, I decided to build my house. My first stop was with the county zoning board. Again, I was surprised and dismayed to learn that the configuration of the lot did not allow for the 70 foot frontage required by the county. My lot is pie shaped with the narrow point facing the street (Ellington Drive). My lot was 60 feet short of meeting the zoning requirements for building. I argued that because a house existed on the lot when I bought it, it seemed logical to me that another house could be built to replace the one the county had forced me to tear down. The county was not cooperative. I went home feeling pretty bad. I had bought a lot and now it appeared I could not put my house on it.

I sat down with the map of the plot and asked myself how I could position the house so as to accommodate the 70 foot frontage requirement. Now, my wife suggested we set the house back off line from the other houses on Ellington Drive when she first saw the lot. Well, I did not think too much of that idea mainly because it would extend our driveway to 130 feet and I thought it would look better online with the other houses. What's more, I was not excited about having 130 feet of snow to shovel every winter. After a while I came up with a plan based on my wife's idea. If I set the house back off the street far enough, I could meet the 70 foot frontage requirement. So I sat down, constructed a map of my building site plan and together with a letter to the zoning board, I set out to fight for a variance to the zoning ordinance. I met with the zoning board, and presented my case. They listened to me and said they would consider it and get back to me with their decision. It took 6 months for them to make a decision. In the meantime I was at the courthouse in

Chinaberry Hill

Upper Marlboro (where the zoning board met) so often some of the employees thought I worked there. I have always believed that if you believe you are right and be aggressive and persistent you will prevail. Well, the zoning board finally ruled in my favor with one caveat. The zoning board would issue a petition to the neighbors on Ellington Drive and if there were no objections, a variance to the zoning rules would be granted and I could build my house. The petition came out in a couple of weeks. I had met a few of my potential neighbors but I had not mentioned my problems with the zoning board. So, I waited and prayed that no one would object. In about three weeks after issuing the petition, I received a letter from the zoning board granting me the variance with the stipulation that my house would have to be placed 130 feet off of Ellington Drive. When I told my wife that we had been given the variance and the house had to be set back 130 feet off of Ellington Drive, she was elated.

The lot is on a hillside. So, in setting it back 130 feet it appeared like "the house on a hill." This pleased my wife very much. I admit it looks very distinguished the way it is positioned but I am still not too hot on shoveling 130 feet of snow.

The next step was to find a builder. Now that builder from whom I purchased the blueprints was out of Pennsylvania and was still in business. However, to my dismay, Beltsville was beyond his building area. He said his building area extended to Baltimore which is about 20 miles North of Beltsville. I did not know that builders had restrictions on the area in which they could build. So, I had to find a local builder. I happen to be talking to one of my coworkers and she mentioned a builder whom she had contacted to do some work for her. She stated that although she decided not to have the work done at that time, the builder appeared to be experienced reliable and had a good reputation in the county. I took the builder's phone number, called him up and made an appointment to meet with him. The company was located in Pasadena, Maryland. A small town about 20 miles East of Beltsville of which I had never heard or visited.

So, I was off to Pasadena. I met with Mandrin Construction Company. We talked. I showed them my blueprints. They said, they did not build that kind of house but asked me to take a look at their catalogue of homes and see if there was anything comparable to the blueprints I had shown them. Well, I reluctantly agreed to look at their catalogue. However, I felt that my wife would be disappointed and would not agree on anything other than the plan we had. Reluctantly, I convinced myself to take a look. To my surprise, I found a house plan that was close enough and had enough floor space to satisfy our needs. Now all I had to do was to convince my wife that this plan was a reasonable substitute for our house plan. I took Mandrin's plans home showed them to my wife and explained the situation to her. I was surprised, she liked Mandrin's house plan and agreed.

I was told by one of my colleagues who had built a custom home not to do it because it was a lot of trouble. Well, I listened to him but I always wanted to build a custom home. However, before our house was finished, I understood what my colleague was saying. There are a lot of challenges inherent in building a custom house but in the end, it is worth the effort. We have a good house suited to our needs that will shelter us for the rest of our life but I will say building a house from scratch is definitely a one-time thing.

COMMENTARY ON LIFE

I don't know what this life's about
This life's too short to sort it out
And so I live from day to day
So at the end my soul can say
I walked this journey sometimes alone
But always moving toward my home
Where darkness rules the day and night
And time and space are infinite
Where bits of ash and dust disperse
To wander through the universe
And by the force of sun and rain
Condense, reform and live again

When I consider all the books that have been written, all the history that has been told and all the science mankind has produced, the beginning and the ending of life and the universe are still a mystery. I believe all life is apart of an intricately connected larger whole. The universe is a dynamic, self-sustaining, self-recycling, self-regenerating and everlasting system. It is directed and controlled by a mighty force that mankind calls by many names. Some even call it God.

If mankind properly regards himself in light of the scope, power and complexity of the universe, he is but a minor blimp on the universe's radar. I believe that long after mankind and all life as we know it have vanished from the earth or anywhere else, the universe will continue. The order power and harmony that exist in the universe did not occur by accident. However, the power and forces that caused it to be are beyond man's ability to fathom. Because mankind is made of and part of the universe and cannot escape from it, his thoughts, plans and being are immersed therein. Therefore, any attempt to find the answer to life or the purpose of the universe will be inherently flawed because it will lack the objectivity necessary to find the truth.

Therefore, I believe we should not waste a lot of time trying to figure out how we got here or what will happen to us when we leave here. Rather, we should spend our time striving to enjoy this beautiful place called earth and the peoples who live thereon. We should work together for peace and prosperity in this world and be sensitive to the suffering of our fellow man. We should develop our talents and use them to make this world a better place in which to live.

Finally, we should love one another and live so when the end comes albeit sometimes untimely, we can say it is well with my soul.

www.ingramcontent.com/pod-product-compliance
Lightning Source LLC
Chambersburg PA
CBHW052134300426
44116CB00010B/1904